A Slice Of Happy

Because the Whole Pie is Overrated

By: Heather A. Korol

First Edition

Some names have been changed in this book to protect the privacy of the individuals portrayed in the stories. Some conversations have been combined from two different time frames for continuity. All opinions expressed in this book are solely the opinion of the author.

Book cover and layout design by Sherry Lemcke.

A Slice of Happy

Because The Whole Pie is Overrated

Heather A. Korol

To Bill Korol (1946-1989), you gave me the courage to ask, “Why not?”

Thank you dad, this slice is for you.

TABLE OF CONTENTS

A Slice of Happy • Because the Whole Pie is Overrated

PREFACE

* * *

I never imagined writing a book would feel like jumping into cold water naked while strangers on shore captured it on their iPhones. *What was I thinking? Why would anyone want to do this?* I wondered these two thoughts repeatedly.

Sitting at my desk, typing stories into the wee hours of the night felt anonymous and liberating; I could hide behind my curtain of words and never experience the reaction of the reader. However, the moment I opened the door to editorial reviews, I felt exposed and vulnerable. It was like yelling to the world, "Judge me!" or "Punch me!" and then standing still while people crushed my ego with a red pen.

Through it all, this book has allowed me to find peace with my thoughts at this stage of my life. I hope it will give a voice to women like myself that want to find a little more happiness on this great journey before it ends.

If I have achieved nothing other than finding my own slice of happy, then I have narcissistically answered my own self-help question: *does it work?* Yes. I started this book because I felt I had something to say and I felt that by saying it, I would be happier. I am. I am happier for having written this book. So thank you, my judging, punching reader, for without you I would be just one more aspiring writer with my clothes on, standing at the edge of the shore holding my iPhone while someone else took the leap.

CHAPTER ZERO

* * *

You can't have it all.

There. I said it.

Our first world, over-informed, 'What's my purpose?' demographic is plagued by this revolving commentary on whether you *can* or *can't* have it all. I'm done with that debate.

A Slice of Happy was written *not* to answer the question, "Can you have it all?" but to answer the question, "If you can't have it all, what can you have?"

I polled a thousand people (okay, maybe thirty) and asked them this question. Most people told me I could have the exact thing they were doing. They said I could have a cup of coffee, a walk on a trail, some crispy bacon, a snort-laugh with a good friend, a sticky hug from a toddler, a bit of shoe-shopping money, or a thrill from completing a long standing project. Some of them said I could have one great accomplishment, or defining achievement in my life. A couple of them told me I could only have "now" – this moment.

I say you can have a slice. I've written the first self-help book to tell you: you can't have it all, but you can have *A Slice of Happy*.

I live in the suburbs of a large city with my husband, three children, and two cats. I'm a business owner. I'm also a coffee-drinking writer, and profanity-using yoga dabbler. I like to sing in my car and the shower. I regularly fantasize about having uninterrupted bathroom time; I think it would feel like transcendence. I also believe every home should have a panic room except I would call mine a napping room. For the last eighteen years I've entertained people with seminars and training programs and I hope to spend the next eighteen years lying on a beach writing about seminars and training programs. Oh, and I like both cats and dogs until I remember that dogs are like toddlers - forever.

I'm not famous, although I wouldn't mind a little taste of it. I'd like just enough to have my hair done for an appearance but not so much that I have to worry if I'm wearing underwear when I get out of a limo. In the spirit of full disclosure, I should mention that I haven't earned a doctorate in psychology, or survived a near death experience that resulted in a celestial being whispering universal truths in my ear. Despite this lack of credibility, I *have* found the secret to happiness.

Believe me, I understand your skepticism about such a statement when there are literally thousands of books about happiness; why would this one be any different? It's different because unlike all the other happiness books, this one has significantly lower expectations. There are no end-of-chapter exercises or goal sheets, no judgments about your life or your lifestyle, and no guilt because you don't recycle, take online courses, or eat organic quinoa. You cannot fail this self-help experiment, because the answer is also conveniently the title.

In the last two decades I've read hundreds of personal, business, and spiritual self-help books in an effort to find this "allness." I attended seminars, set goals, followed action steps, used time blocks, breathed, chakra'd, networked, and meditated, in an effort to find the right formula. I've both succeeded and failed yet I repeatedly came to the same conclusion:

I couldn't put all the pieces together at the same time.

I found that as I grabbed every savory bit of one life slice, another slice was slipping through my fingers into the bin of unrealized dreams. Excelling in my career and then starting a family was like crashing a test car into a wall and hoping the dummy would come away unscathed. Being a dedicated mother with both the time and energy to enjoy my children resulted in a body I didn't recognize and the hours once spent socializing with friends had been replaced with catching up on work due to a more demanding schedule and a failing economy. Twenty years have passed since I started this journey towards a "better me" and I'm not sure if I've awakened my giant within or simply nudged the slightly-larger-than-average person I've become.

A Slice of Happy is about a woman, perhaps like so many other women - that somewhere between catapulting into life at twenty and slamming into forty, lost some of her happy along the way. It's the story about loving goals, dreams, and adventures but living a life of schedules, demands, and unrealistic expectations.

In a world filled with seemingly unlimited opportunity, I came to understand that you can't have it all, that happiness is a feeling not an accomplishment, and that finding your own slice of happy is a matter of knowing where to get started.

A Slice of Happy is how I found happiness through focus rather than distraction, through perspective rather than achievement. It's about how I put aside the "have-tos" and the "shoulds" in exchange for the passion of indulging in one thing that made me feel, happy.

PART I

The Whole Pie

CHAPTER ONE

* * *

What Do You Mean, I Can't Have It All?

I didn't just wake up one morning and realize that I couldn't have it all. It crept up slowly like the fine lines around my eyes and how yoga pants had become my new jeans. For years, I assumed that with enough hard work and perseverance, I would be enjoying financial freedom, career advancement, Zen-like patience, toned abs, angelic children, a charitable constitution, and uncluttered closets—the whole pie. I believed if I dug in, set a goal, and rallied the just-do-it spirit, I would turn the corner and find a giant happy pie in my kitchen.

I talked to my best friend about finding this pie.

"Tina, I was at yoga yesterday. I swear some of the women eat Botox for breakfast. I heard one of them talking about going on a cruise with her *whole* family."

"That sounds terrible."

"What, eating Botox or going on a cruise with your kids and in-laws?"

"Both. At least Botox would make me look younger. Going on a cruise with my kids would age me ten years." We both had toddlers, which meant the word *vacation* was code for sleepless relocation.

"I know. How do people get promoted at work, go on vacations, eat homemade dehydrated kale chips, and still find time to work in a soup kitchen every third Sunday? Where's this secret happy-tree that grows money and pukes life fulfillment?"

"Ugh. I wish I knew. Maybe everyone is faking it?"

"They are, I'm sure of it. What if people had to post their honest vacation photos to Facebook? Kids screaming in the car, an eye-dagger fight with your spouse at the departure gate, and someone with the flu the minute you arrive?" I asked.

"Happy vacation photos are one part fact and three parts fiction."

"Exactly. Life is fractional: a quarter awesome, two parts average, and one part crappy. What if all you ever get is a slice?"

"Like a slice of life?" Tina questioned.

"Yes, but more like a happy slice. Look how we are constantly trying to get more things done, make more money, lose weight, and for what? To make it appear like we have everything under control, all the time? What if all you ever get is a slice—a slice of happy?" I paused while I tried to find an example of someone that had it all. "I mean, really, name one of our friends who has the perfect life, the whole pie?"

"What about your friend Kristen? Big house, nice husband, good kids," Tina asked.

"Okay, but she's miserable. She never sees her husband because he's working all the time, and she's lonely."

"All right, what about your friends John and Micah?"

"Nope—dying to have kids. Classic infertility life crusher."

"Yeah, I guess. But if all you ever get is a slice, or even a sliver, would that be okay?"

"It would *have* to be, because that's all you might ever get." I paused while the inevitable question percolated from my brain to my mouth, "Tina, what if we can't have it all?"

She breathed out a long sigh, "Maybe that would be easier."

That's when my realization stopped creeping and slammed me in the face, like my toddler smashing my nose while I put on her shoes.

I couldn't have it all.

I know it sounds naive, but I was shocked by this revelation. I felt cheated. I was certain that with enough "Dream, Dare, Do!" from the land of self-help, positive-thinking gurus that with enough hard work, the complete package would be mine. For so many years I had believed I could have it all, the whole pie, that I honestly never thought to question whether it was possible.

The Whole Pie or Just a Slice?

If you've ever attended a motivational seminar or a self-help getaway, the leader will often talk about your life like it's a pie. Standing at the flip-chart easel, he or she will say, "Thiiiis is your life." And with the squeak of a marker, the leader will draw a giant circle. "Your life is this circle. Now give me some areas in your life that you feel are important." Someone in the group might say, "My kids."

"Okay, good—kids. That would be the family section."

Then the leader will draw two lines in the circle, like a slice of pie, and boldly label the slice "family."

"All right, another area of importance?"

"My job!"

"Great! Let's call that the career slice." Another line is drawn on the pie. This continues until the pie is sliced up with all the key areas of people's lives. Self-help leaders love to talk about these sections that constitute the wheel or pie of life. The slices include health, wealth, relationships, career, community, spirituality, leisure, and family—the standard eight areas addressed in motivational seminars. They carve up your life pie and dissect your contentedness based on the number of full slices. If all your slices are filled up, then in theory you have the whole pie, and who doesn't want that? Who doesn't want each day full of meditating, hugging, recycling, charitable giving, work fulfillment, profitable ventures, contented life partners, fantastical sex, and responsible children?

I certainly tried.

In an attempt to achieve success in all the slices at once, I found life's pesky roadblocks could derail my progress in an instant. Spending quality time with my three children feels magical until I realize no one has made dinner and we have parent teacher interviews in twenty minutes. Being connected to nature fills me with awe, except when I'd rather dive into a pool of DEET then be devoured by a plague of mosquitoes. How can anyone feel a sense of accomplishment, a sense of happiness when a portion of your life disappears into the vortex of insanity, as you debate charges on your cell phone with a person in customer service you've never met but wouldn't mind choking through the phone.

True happiness has become confused with completing items on a to-do list; it has become lost in a competition over who owns the most stuff and sadly, I believe happiness has been downgraded from a very attainable goal to a "pie in the sky" life fantasy.

Most people want the whole-pie of happiness, I did; but what if all you ever get is one really great slice at a time? What if happiness is found *not* by spreading yourself so thin that you don't have the time or energy to focus on any one thing, but true happiness is found when you pick a slice and roll around in the filling until it seeps into your soul like a giant anti-aging mask? One slice, one focus.

You would feel full, satisfied, and maybe even happy.

CHAPTER TWO

* * *

Who Am I to Tell You How To Be Happy?

I get it. Who am I to tell you how to find happiness?

Probably like you, I dream of being, doing, and having just a little bit more—a little more money, a little more love, and a little more happiness. Call it the bucket list, life goals, or self-help—I think about new challenges, both big and small, and I get excited.

Fifteen years ago I would have paid a lot of money to be coached by one of my self-help heroes. At the time, every one of their answers would have seemed perfect, but I wonder how I would I feel now. How would their suggestions affect me today, outside the bubble of youth and endless optimism?

I often catch myself daydreaming what it would be like if the triad of self-help demigods—Tony Robbins, Oprah, and the Dalai Lama—showed up at my house, the one with three kids, a husband, and nine bikes in the garage. What would happen if they left their ivory towers of enlightenment and joined me on my quest to get out the door on a Monday morning?

A Day in the Life with Tony, Oprah, the Dalai Lama, and Me

As Tony Robbins hands me my first cup of steaming organic tea, I glance at my life goals poster board hanging above the kitchen sink. It's filled with cutouts of toned, slightly emaciated women, mattresses made of money, and tropical island retreats. A picture of my head is taped on top of the model's body so I can envision my new look, while I manifest financial freedom. I'm supposed to be aspiring to become the real life version of my poster board. All I can think about is how this tea kind of sucks compared to my morning coffee. Tony is eager to get me started on unleashing my power within.

TONY: "Okay, Heather, now close your eyes and really visualize where you see yourself five years from now. Don't just think about it; really feel it. Try to hear it. Even try to smell it."

ME: "Listen, Tony, I know you are the world's best coach but if I close my eyes, this machine called the morning routine will grind to a halt. And really? How can anyone visualize anything without coffee?"

TONY: "Let's stay in the *now*, Heather. Let's use our neural linguistic programming. No more 'if-then,' 'what if,' or 'someday I'll.' Say it like you mean it! Say 'I AM!' Say 'I HAVE!' How can you possibly see yourself living your dreams if your words are fraught with negatives and diminishing self-talk?"

ME: "Language, right. Okay, I put my affirmation worksheet on the fridge behind the kids field trip permission forms, under the Pizza Pizza magnet."

When I glance across the room, I see Oprah sitting at my kitchen table.

O: "Girrrrl. Come over here and sit down. Three kids, your own business, and now you're writing a book. Get over here and take a load off!"

ME: "Oh, Oprah. (*Sigh.*) I love you. Clara! Ellie! Fiona! Get in here! It's Oprah, the greatest female role model in the last hundred years. GET IN HERE! Now be quiet and grateful. Oprah says that every day must start with gratitude."

It's then that I realize why she's asked me to sit down. It dawns on me: she's taped a set of new car keys underneath my kitchen chair. Oh. My. God. Oprah is here to give me a new car so I can fit all three car seats in at one time. I can't contain myself. I have to look. I bend over, reach my hand under the chair, and feel around. I get down on my knees and peer up at the seat belly, straining to see the key ring or envelope I know the keys are in.

O: "What are you looking for, honey?"

ME: "Uh—car keys...for the new car in my driveway?"

O: "New car? Well, that certainly would be something to be grateful for, but you only get a new car if you *do* something. All those people on my show did something, like save dying animals in a tsunami, or read books to blind children, or take blankets and homemade cookies to people that live on the streets. Heck, some of them even give up their own kidneys to dying strangers. What have you done? Let's do a little work on giving before receiving. Think of me as your gratitude coach."

ME: "Okay, you're right. Just let me pack all the lunches, get the library books, and drop a wad of cash in each kid's backpack so they can support the 'give money every day to some charity at school' program. Oh, and Oprah, can you be careful with those Jimmy Choos near the baby? Thanks."

I love Oprah. I love Tony. But the next man I see in my house is quite possibly the greatest physical manifestation of love. I leave Oprah with her egg whites, only to find the Chosen One on my living room couch. I'm not entirely sure how you greet the Dalai Lama.

ME: "Hello, Your Holiness." I'm not a Buddhist, but I sure did love your book, *The Art of Happiness.*

As I shove the kids toward the door and jam backpacks, hats, mittens, boots, and scarves on their little frames, I realize that the Dalai Lama is probably not going to be super chatty. His silence is my cue to ask him some questions.

ME: "Your Holiness, how can I live a life of greatness when I suffer the burdens of being middle class? I am the tax resource for the rich and charitable bank for the poor. Can you offer me some advice?"

DL: "You must not class yourself as one or the other. You are a soul that is free to choose. You have chosen this path. You need only choose again."

ME: "Kids! Get walking! Out the door now or you'll be late! Sorry, Mr. Lama. Okay, so I just need to un-choose what I have, and then my pettiness will be lessened and I can find inner peace?"

DL: "Yespf, thiff ith da pafth to fahlow."

ME: "Oh, my. Are you speaking to me in tongues? Are you guiding me to inner peace?"

As I wait, I notice his jaw moving, but he is not saying anything. I'm perplexed. I think he may be channeling a higher voice through himself to speak to me. I wait patiently as he moves his hand toward his side.

ME: "Hey, what's in your robe? Are you eating Skittles? Are those the kid's peanut-free treats from their lunch bags?" Oh, lord.

DL: "You must find peace within your children's generosity. They most graciously offered me their sweets."

Me: "Thanks." I imagine the headline: *Kids give candy to Dalai Lama—Mother wins award for teaching selflessness.*

Sigh. If there isn't a mantra that can cure the Buddha incarnate from being a sugar addict, how can he help a mother of three who just wants her thighs not to touch when she walks? Your Holiness, please help me. Guide me, save me, open my eyes to the windows of life, and for Buddha's sake, let me wear a robe to work every day.

Self-help Happy

Well meaning self-help gurus give the illusion that change is as easy as thinking, writing, or breathing your way to a new you. According to Marketdata Enterprises, in 2009 the US self-improvement market was worth over ten billion dollars.[1] This is a lot of self-help; but do the motivational books, seminars, programs, DVDs, and other products that profess to lead us to nirvana work? Can you be saved from your addictions, unhealthy habits, and relationship problems by following their scripted formulas?

The answer is yes.

And no.

The world of self-help is a maze filled with various paths to the cheese. If you buy a book on de-cluttering and the first chapter tells you to throw things out, and you do, then it worked, or at the very least it helped. If a book offers you a mantra for inner peace, and when you invoke this word charm you feel calm, then some part of the program worked for you. Who cares what people think? If a book helps you on a path to becoming a better *you*, celebrate. If you feel more content, more peaceful, or happier because of these changes, then your efforts will have been worth it.

And no, self-help doesn't work. Not the way gurus want you to believe. Self-help programs create a vision for you and give you steps to go from the bottom rung to pie-in-the-sky success. It always sounds simple, but when you start on your new program you realize you've been given a step stool and not an escalator. Instead of rocketing to the top; as seen on the infomercial, most people end up stopping a few steps from where they started. Incredible self-help transformations like you see on TV or in magazines don't often happen, because most people don't change that much. The work, energy, and process involved to reach the top rung is enormous, and most people become content after they've elevated themselves one or two steps.

It's obvious I'm not Tony, Oprah or the Dalai Lama but I hope that my story, will inspire you find your own slice of happy. The next page is filled with a list of my successes and if this sounds self-aggrandizing and irritating to you, rest assured that the page after that is filled with a list of my failures.

My Perfect Pie

In 1989, I was a budding track star in the 100-meter hurdles and the long jump. I earned a four-year track and field scholarship to Northern Arizona University. I raced, studied (and partied) my way through university and in 1994, I graduated All-American with a double major in chemistry and microbiology. I walked across an elaborate fake-flowered stage, received my diploma, flipped my hat tassel, and it was all over in a blink. At least now it feels like a blink. Back then it felt like I lived in a shoebox with never ending lab classes, and only enough money to split a pizza with five other people.

As I packed my bags to leave the United States and return to the sprawling suburb of Mississauga (located in balmy, South Central Canada), I realized I was leaving the safety net of school schedules and syllabi. I was effectively ending the chapter called 'student-life' and starting the chapter called 'real life.' For the first time in twenty years, I wouldn't have a timeline, a schedule, or a predetermined set of goals created by an institution with guidelines and regulations. As eternal as the university process seemed, it ended without fanfare – or a life map.

I flew home with a sense of excitement and anxiety. I would finally be in charge of my life. Every-little-bit-of-it.

With a degree suited to lab work and no desire to work in a lab, I had to find work. At twenty-two I started my own business. I borrowed $6000 from a big-box electronic store, I bought a laptop that weighed eight pounds, a portable printer, and a cell phone the size of my shoe. I started Results Training - one of the first personal training businesses that offered in-home, Hollywood-style training. I made average people feel like superstars as I purged their fridges and helped them tighten their glutes.

I paid off my debt within six months, expanded to five employees, and cracked the six-figure income within three years.

By 1997, I was ready for a new challenge. I packed up and moved to a tropical island for eighteen months. I learned Spanish and opened a clothing store. I bought a condo on the ocean with the money from my training business and envisioned an early retirement. I was twenty-six.

By 2001 I had completed two of the toughest adventure races in the world, The Southern Traverse and Raid the North Extreme. These races were grueling, multi-day team events covering distances of over 600 kilometers from start to finish. As a team we reached the podium in our own country and placed well abroad.

My training, racing, and business experience allowed me to excel at a speaking career where I promoted goal-setting and action steps in both health and business topics to fortune 500 companies both in Canada and the USA.

I dared people to make changes in their physical well-being as well as their career choices.

In 2005, I married a wonderful man and through our mutual love of adventures we started an events company. Our company, Hark Events Inc. grew until we successfully owned and operated five large races.

Within the next seven years we had three beautiful children, sold our first house, and bought our second home in the resort town of Collingwood. In 2010, we sold our events company and now I spend my days writing and preparing for seminars that I deliver around the country.

It sounds like I have the whole pie – a great career, incredible adventures, loving family, and expendable income. I would like to say that this is the entire story but like most people, there were trade-offs.

My Reality Pie

I returned home from university in the recession of the early 1990s. I couldn't find a job anywhere. When I started my personal training company I also worked nights at a bar called Don Cherry's Sports Grill. I closed my shift at 3am only to start working with clients at 6am. The amount of training I did with these clients made me physically sick. I was exhausted. I never went out or did anything other than work. The more money I made, the more challenges I faced with staffing, budgets, accounting, and general management of the business. I found running a business debilitating.

In my distress, I went on vacation and fell in love with the idea that life could be like living on a resort. I moved to the Dominican Republic in an attempt to escape the pressure of around-the-clock work stress. I learned to speak marginal Spanish which made me not-quite-fluent-enough to understand the complex social and business mores of a developing country. Despite my best effort to run a profitable clothing store, I lost $80,000 in a country that only had electricity on Mondays, Wednesdays, and Fridays. Within eighteen months I moved back to Canada, my island dream washed away.

When I returned to my athletic roots in the form of adventure racing, I raced with a team that acted more like a dysfunctional family than a cohesive unit and although we finished well, the adventures took their toll on my bank account, my body and my psyche.

I got married after we had our first baby and while this isn't uncommon, we faced an uphill battle as our first-born was more difficult than the average newborn. Clara was later diagnosed with sensory integration disorder, a lifetime miscommunication between the brain and the external senses that make normal day-to-day functions seem insurmountable. Raising three kids and managing the extra demands of a 'sensory child' added additional stress to our home life. Ten years of building our events company created tremendous pressure around race deadlines. The seemingly glamorous title of 'race director' entailed thousands of hours of logistic planning in front of spreadsheet that made my head hurt daily. I managed all of the events through each pregnancy, and because I ran my own business, I didn't receive any maternity leave benefits. I gained weight, struggled with mortgage payments, and wondered if balancing all these tasks with the needs of our growing family would ever get easier. Our move to a new town required my husband to have a longer commute and we sold our events company at a time when the economy was not exceptionally positioned to sustain a writing and speaking career.

Domestically I'm a mess. My cupboard doors hide a secret world of chaos; laundry is piled high enough to pose as furniture and I often serve breakfast foods for dinner. We own a car that is eleven years old and an SUV that is eight years old. We live in a large house with an equally large mortgage and even when every bit of parenting information suggests otherwise, I still yell at my kids.

Throughout my life, my happiness chart has looked like a seismic graph of an earthquake prone area; there are jagged, high peaks of happiness and squashy, fat lulls of dissatisfaction. The goal achieving pattern of climbing and falling, climbing and jumping, wrong goals, someone else's goals, great achievements, and moderate successes are what opened my eyes to my inability to achieve happiness in all areas of my life. There was a reappearing theme: the cost of succeeding or finding happiness in one area of life came at the price of another.

Here I was, a woman that had started more than one successful business, lived on an island, climbed mountains, and inspired audiences with her life choices and yet I still felt like I was just getting by. I craved better connections, greater depth in my conversations, and more quality time with my kids. I longed to feel like I made difference, that my ideas mattered - that my existence mattered. I wanted to feel more alive.

No one seems to be immune.

If you are in a great personal relationship, you may be struggling to find a satisfying career. If your career is flying high, the working hours you need to remain successful may eat into the time you have with your family. Maybe you are blessed with a fulfilling career and a body that is your temple, but you are searching to find the right person to share it with. Perhaps you've unlocked the secret to spiritual growth, but this has led you to a direct conflict with finding meaningful work or a suitable life partner. Or ironically, you may be in a fantastic relationship, have an advancing career, an incredible family, and achieve transcendent spiritual calm, only to visit your doctor and find you are knocking on death's door.

People travel the globe, bathe in hot springs, walk to Mecca, climb the tallest mountain, and still don't find it all. Like Tom Cruise to Cuba Gooding Jr. in *Jerry Maguire*, I scream in the bathroom to the world, "SHOW ME THE WHOLE PIE!"

So, who am I to tell you how to be happy? I'm a person probably not so unlike yourself. I have a list of successes and a list of failures. When I looked at my life, I couldn't stop thinking that *I* was the problem; *I* wasn't trying hard enough or following the right steps. I couldn't have it all because *I* wasn't doing it right.

I was constantly waiting for everything to come together. I was waiting for a time when we had enough money to relax - even though we were in the most demanding years of raising a family. I was waiting for someone to discover my speaking talent - even though I was hiding in my office working on an event spreadsheet. I was waiting for my fat to melt away after our third baby - even though I found a row of cookies a good excuse for dinner. I was waiting to take a deep breath, turn the corner, and find the whole pie.

I will never tell anyone that they shouldn't try to better themselves, set personal goals, or want more out of life. But as I've tested my own limits, I continually come back to the same philosophy: the whole pie is earthly nirvana. It's every hope, dream, and desire we have for ourselves but our life pie is made up of the slices: health, wealth, career, family, relationship, community, leisure, and spirituality. Each slice has a place and time in your life and the amount of focus you will be able to give to each one will ebb and flow.

As my pie plate filled up with career, family, expenses and social obligations, I realized that being focused on *one area* equaled a level of contentment I couldn't find when I tried to do everything all at once. I knew I was done trying to have the whole pie because I finally believed it wasn't possible. I stopped trying to make my life fit into an unrealistic formula. I was ready to choose one slice and pour my energy into making it great.

I was finally ready to be happier, one slice at a time.

Heather Korol

OCCUPATION:

Motivational Speaker and Personal Fitness Trainer
Pinnacle Fitness, Oakville, Ont.

TECHNOLOGY:

Zenith Z-Noteflex laptop • Canon Bubble Jet BJC-70 color printer • Motorola cell phone on Cantel

Heather Korol is a motivational speaker and personal fitness trainer whose mobile technology can only barely keep up with her pace and schedule. She has her own company called Pinnacle Fitness and does seminars, fitness training and appraisals for corporations (such as employees of Royal Insurance, Nesbitt Burns and Ontario Hydro), as well as personal training for individuals.

Korol lives the busy lifestyle her clients have, and she practises what she preaches. Some days she trains as many as seven clients a day from high level managers to hard-core marathoners. On other days she's leading seminars in conference rooms.

After graduating from Northern Arizona University with a B.Sc. in biochemistry (on a track and field scholarship) [illegible]

out a report and seeing it on paper, brings it to life. It's hard to ignore the facts when they are staring you in the face," she says. "But if I gathered the information, had to go away to input it and print it, and then meet with the person another time, my chances of [illegible]

positive attitude, Korol believes in changing her voice-mail message every day. "I think people should always make their message lively and upbeat. Tell people where you are or when you can be reached so it sounds fresh every time they hear you," says Korol.

Article from En Route Magazine, 1997. Cell phone the size of a shoe.

CHAPTER THREE

* * *

Stuff-Stuff-Stuff

Am I happy? Of course I'm happy. Except when I'm miserable. If you heard me on the phone chatting, you would think I lived in the 1800s and was out chopping wood all day so I could cook bone soup on an open hearth, darn socks, hope for rain, gather mushrooms, and find leeches for a quick bloodletting. But I don't. I live in suburbia and I'm surrounded by problems that stem from forgetting my log-in password, being invaded by high fructose corn syrup, and bedtime routines that require forty-five minutes of dedicated calmness.

Finding happiness is not rocket science, it's not even science-science. *Happiness is a feeling.* It is not something to be acquired. It is not a place, a purchase, or a reward; it is not an island vacation, a new car, or a career promotion—it is a feeling. It's easy to forget that happiness is an emotion that we *feel* when pervasive marketing campaigns tell us happiness is measured in carats or square footage.

Stuff You Already Know

Over the years, I've learned there are two common themes that keep people from being happier: having too much stuff and comparing all of that stuff to other people's stuff.

We all live with too much stuff that doesn't make us happy. I'm not just talking about physical stuff, but *all* of the stuff we collect in our lives: people, emotions, negative experiences. We carry them around like badges of honor. We proudly proclaim, "Oh, look at all my life's baggage. Look how much stuff I have, how much I have struggled, and how I've packed it in these industrial-strength suitcases so that I can build a fortress with my pain."

And other people's stuff: when we are not processing all of our stuff, we are comparing our stuff to other people's stuff. We compare physical things, like our houses, cars, furniture, and gadgets. We compare our experiences, like our marriages, jobs, kids, and relationships. We even compare our future potential, like how long we might live, how healthy we may be, or how we might feel when we retire.

When you compare your stuff to other people's stuff, only one of two things can happen:

1. You feel worse about yourself.
2. You feel worse about other people.

You don't need a degree in human nature to know that we do this constantly. We rank ourselves on a giant universal scale that says, "I'm better off than you" or "I'm worse off than you."

We compare and we judge. We wonder if their stuff is better than ours, worse than ours, or leads us to greater or lesser life satisfaction. We judge other people's decisions, actions, words, dreams, and choices. It doesn't matter where you live, how much money you have, or any other factor involved in finding happiness. Too much stuff makes us unhappy and comparing our stuff to others' makes us downright miserable.

Everyone has their own Achilles' heel when it comes to judging others. It's the one area that brings out the worst in our personality. I suffer from piles-of-stuff shame. I don't care if people have nice cars, dream vacations, or stacks of cash. My self-esteem plummets when I enter the domicile of the organized person. Recently I walked into an acquaintance's house for the first time and thought she was selling her home. I wondered when the sign was going up on the lawn.

"Are you guys listing your house?"

"No, why?"

"Oh. Um, it's just that it's so organized and, well, clean."

Please help me. I hate these people. I'm jealous and they ruin my day. I secretly think there's something horribly wrong with the rest of their lives if they have this much time to be organized. When my husband and I put our house up for sale, I spent seventeen days cleaning, sorting, and de-cluttering. I hung pictures that had never seen a wall. I fixed, painted, and tossed out enough stuff to open a store. It was exhausting and overwhelming and I'm sure it took ten times the effort an organized person would have needed. I hired cleaners and the best full commission real-estate agent I could find, and I commandeered any available relative to help pack up or hide piles of stuff. Each day I called my best friend to moan about the process. When we were ready to put up the for sale sign, my house looked like other people's houses look every day. EVERY DAY. How is this possible? How is it that I am so inadequate at the process of running and organizing my life that I needed full-time help and therapy to get our house ready for sale?

See? Comparing and judging. I'm in a new house now. I'm trying. My best bet is to put this one up for sale in a couple of years, before I meet all the neighbors with their toaster-free counters, organized fridge shelves, and plastic storage bins for seasonal clothing.

There is hope. If the word 'comparison' is the nemesis of happiness, then there is one word that can be the hero to happiness; if comparison hurts, then *perspective* heals.

Perspective Should Be Worn Daily, Like Underwear and Sunscreen

The glass is half full, the glass is half empty, or the glass is a container that holds water; it's all about perspective. When I look at my life, it's easy to see these three different perspectives:

1. I have three children, a loving husband, and a beautiful home, and I joyously write for a living.
2. I have three dependents. I'm bound to another human for life. I have a twenty-five-year mortgage and no job security or retirement plan.
3. We decided to have kids. I picked this person to share my life with. My home is where I live, and I write because I can.

It really just depends on where you stand. If you are standing outside of my shoes, you might see nothing but the perfect life. If you stood in my shoes—or better yet, my filing cabinet—this so-called perfect life would look radically different. The truth lies somewhere in the middle. We all need perspective, because sometimes our stuff gets in the way of seeing what's important.

My husband and I often spend time with a wonderful couple. They are kind, honest, and fun. They have two teenage kids and a small house with one bathroom. There isn't a piece of furniture or paint color in their home that is younger than me. They always invite us for dinner, and they don't have a dishwasher. They *never* wash the dishes while we are there. It's clear to me that they enjoy family, friends, and nature.

Recently we dropped over for a visit.

"Hey, you guys made it! We're glad you brought the kids, we love seeing them."

They like our kids? I don't even like our kids.

"What can we get you to drink?"

Jason and his wife Laura are what you would call happy people. Not happy in the "let me show you our new giant television" way, but in a way that says everyone can have a moment to shine.

"What are you guys doing this weekend?" I asked, because they often have something going on.

"Oh, it's our annual back-country canoe trip with the family."

Planning a trip like this seems like a supreme accomplishment, considering their kids are fifteen and seventeen, an age when they might not be interested in spending a week with their parents portaging and tenting. "That's great. Are you looking forward to it?" I asked with genuine interest.

"Of course, we love it."

That was it. They loved it. I had nothing to say, because they would never understand why I wouldn't love that kind of trip. They wouldn't get my complaint about not wanting to make a five-hour drive without a smartphone or iPad for each kid, because they didn't have them at all. They wouldn't get my mental debate about what food to pack, because their kids would just eat whatever was being served. I could never go with my family for an extended canoe trip because, after what it would take to get everyone organized, I would probably yell "Wait!" and jump behind the car in the hope that my husband would run me over so I wouldn't have to go. It wouldn't matter if it was canoeing in the backcountry or a five-star trip to Disneyland—all of it seems like too much, and it all seems easier for people like Laura and Jason.

When I come home to our sprawling house, my new quartz counter top, our super-silent dishwasher, and fridge-door ice machine, I feel like a big fat fake. I feel like I've forgotten the most important things in life: family, friends, and nature. As I proceed to fill my cup with ready-made ice and water, put my glass in the dishwasher, and sit at my kitchen island, I wonder: am I really *this* person, or do I secretly desire to be *those* people?

Do I really care what other people have, think, or do? Would living in a perfectly organized house make me happy, or would it make me crazy? Is it okay for my kids to play outside unsupervised, or am I less caring than the helicopter mom down the street? I play the comparative life game constantly, and I play it to the detriment of my happiness. It's become clear to me that too much stuff makes me miserable and comparing my stuff to other people's stuff makes me feel inadequate. When I remember to seek out perspective and quiet the obnoxious, judging voice in my head, I know I am happier.

Happy U

According to an economist from the University of Michigan, the more times you recognize your happiness, the greater your overall happiness will be.[2] That's good because I have a list taped to my desk that includes petting kittens, drinking coffee, and sleeping under a duvet but when I stumbled on the latest research about life happiness I was dismayed by the findings. I called Tina to see if it made sense to her.

"Hey, Tina. I read this article that said we are most unhappy at the age of forty-four. I'm forty-one years old. According to research, in three years I will be the unhappiest I've ever been."

"What do you mean? Does it say that suddenly at age forty-four we become unhappy, like we fall into a pit of misery?" Tina sounded shocked by this information.

"No, it's more like a slow decline until you hit bottom at forty-four. Then you start to climb out of your unhappiness until you're about seventy-four. After that, it says, decrepitude and ailments make you miserable again."

"Really? That's depressing. I'm thirty-seven. You're saying that I have seven more years of declining happiness until the ball starts to roll uphill?"

"That's what it says. Here's the irony: the graph has a high point on the far left side when you are seven years old and then an equally high point when you are seventy. It dips to the bottom when you're forty-four. It's shaped like a smile, like a damned happy face."

According to this research, I was now facing three more years of declining happiness, but my new mantra was fresh on my lips – pick a slice and enjoy it. I was ready to find my slice, no matter what the research was extolling.

If I was going to find my slice of happy, I needed to know what that meant to me. Just as most people are not mad, glad, angry, or sad all the time, they are also not happy all the time. Just as we have varying degrees of negative emotions, we have varying levels of happiness. I have found there are three distinct levels of happiness and I wanted them all.

Hollywood Happy

Hollywood happy is big, giant, obvious to everyone including yourself happiness. Hollywood happiness feels like a gushing, proud day that is usually accompanied by a card that says 'Congratulations!" on your new job, wedding, or other grand accomplishment. These are the lifetime achievement awards of happiness; the feelings associated with them can be linked to emotional outbursts, like whooping and clapping or making a heart-warming speech. Most people can both recognize this happy feeling and the associated accomplishment it was derived from.

Engaged Happy

Engaged happiness is a gloriously deep, satisfied feeling. It often comes from doing something that allows you to become completely absorbed in the task at hand. Painting, writing, hiking, or cooking may be activities that give you such immense satisfaction that it feels like minutes have passed when it's really been hours. Engaged happiness is usually connected with a verb like running, playing, writing or socializing, and it fills you with both intensity and inner contentment.

Heavenly Happy

Heavenly happiness is a feeling that is hard to describe because it feels like pure joy. It has been my experience that the smaller the moment of recognition the more profound the feeling. It could be a blink of time or breath of air; it could be a moment of calm. Heavenly happiness could strike while you are alone in your car, it could be while you are attending a function or it could happen in the busiest airport with people all around you; this happiness is felt in a moment where life seems perfect.

Martin Luther King Jr. captured the experience with these words: "Occasionally in life there are those moments of unutterable fulfillment which cannot be completely explained by those symbols called words. Their meanings can only be articulated by the inaudible language of the heart."[3]

Picking my slice had to come from a place that would allow me to feel happiness on all three levels. I needed to check off the Hollywood happiness box because I knew I was looking for an element of accomplishment. I also wanted to feel engaged happiness, as I wanted to feel immersed in whatever activity I chose to pursue. And ultimately I wanted to feel a sense of connection to something greater than myself; I wanted my choice to feel a little bit, heavenly.

I was ready to pick my slice.

Getting ready to sell our house in 2011. My linen closet before and after.

PART II

My Slice

CHAPTER FOUR

* * *

Eeny, Meeny, Miny, Pie

I felt like kid in a pie store. There were so many slices that I wanted to taste that picking one was a challenge. I wanted to lose weight, focus on my career, give the best to my children, and I wanted to find out first hand if having more money was a blessing or a curse. I needed to pick a slice that would hit me with a flavor burst, excite me, and leave me feeling full and satiated. I decided on a systematic approach to narrow down which one I would choose. I looked at all the pieces - health, wealth, community, leisure, family, relationships, career, and spirituality - and I started to prioritize. I tossed the ones that had no immediate appeal, and then I used a combination of logical and emotional arguments to see which one would make the cut.

I eliminated the community slice on the first round. With small children and financial pressures, I didn't feel I had the time or energy to focus on this slice.

The spirituality slice was next. I had spent a fair bit of time in my twenties exploring my faith and examining my beliefs so I felt this slice could also be put on hold.

Next, I took out the leisure slice. Before kids, I did my share of traveling and adventure seeking, I was pretty sure a big bungee jump or skydive wasn't going to give me the happiness satisfaction I was seeking, so goodbye leisure slice.

The next two required more consideration.

With a deep breath, I put the family slice next on the chopping block. This one pressed my guilt button. I've been a work-from-home mom since my children were born. Balancing being an available parent to my children and being prepared for my work has been a fly by the seat of my pants experience. The stress of trying to keep it all together has been less than satisfying. The number of times I'd juggled my work and home schedules, trying to make everything happen, created an unhappiness that was reflected in the distracted way I was parenting my children. By *not* choosing the family slice, I felt that my parenting skills might actually get better. If I was able give myself the permission to let go of being the primary responder to my kids' needs, I felt I would be able to better enjoy the time I spent with them. I knew I would still be an involved parent, but I also knew I was ready to delegate as many tasks as needed to focus on something other than the family slice. I love my family slice dearly, but this slice is wearing me out.

After some careful thought, I ruled out the relationship slice. My husband and I have already weathered the hard years of raising small children: the years when sleep is worth more than gold and everyone in the house trades viruses like Pokémon cards. As the kids have gotten older, we've been able to find more time to be together as a couple. I felt secure that I could take this slice out of the running.

This still left me with my health, wealth, and career slices. These were three choices that got me excited. Each one offered great rewards if I chose to focus on it. I knew I wanted to feel Hollywood, engaged, and heavenly happiness but I had to figure out which one of the three would give me those feelings.

Health

I've been an athlete all my life but today, I don't look like an athlete. I look like an active mom. You would never mistake me for the person I used to look like. Having had our third baby months before my fortieth birthday turned out to be tougher than I expected on my body. I always thought I would bounce back after each pregnancy but there's no rule that says just because you used to be super fit doesn't mean you are exempt from gaining weight due to pregnancy, life stress, and aging. I hated feeling this way.

An essential part of who I have been all my life is tied up with my body shape and my health. I knew that if I got back into fantastic shape, I would not only feel good, I would feel confident. Picking the health slice could lead me back to training people, and new clients would lead to increased income. This slice could have a lot of positive affects.

On the negative side, focusing on my health slice would take me back in time. I'd already spent many years dedicated to this slice and I wasn't sure if being an athlete was who I wanted to be again. I would be trading career or wealth opportunities for my health slice and I wasn't sure if I cared that much about my body fat anymore.

The health slice was in the running but I still needed to think about the other two.

Wealth

The wealth slice: who doesn't want more of this piece of pie? Plain and simple, focusing on the wealth slice would mean having more money and I liked that idea. Before kids, I had a much larger expendable income and it made a lot of things easier. My motto was: *Got a problem? Throw some money at it.* The thought of having more income was very appealing considering the amount of money needed to keep our house and family afloat.

On the positive side, focusing on the wealth slice wouldn't require a career adjustment; it would only require earning more income doing what I was already doing. For me, this could mean securing a few contract positions with events companies or seeking out new sponsors for the events we already managed. I could also include taking the time to ensure we were focused on sticking to our budget and holding onto the savings we already had put away.

Having extra money would relieve immediate financial strains, it would make me feel secure, and it would take away the stress of running my own business but it would also mean working for other people, increased travel time, and less flexibility with my family schedule. The wealth slice had it's benefits, but it wouldn't come without a cost.

Career

Like most people the career slice is one that defines our unique talents or abilities. When you feel like you aren't living up to your own expectations, this slice is a very enticing choice.

Twenty years ago, my best friend Tina and I co-wrote an idea for a book. The book was titled *Why You Suck...at Finding a Job.* The book series was to be titled *Why You Suck* and included a range of topics: why you suck at finding love, losing weight, getting rich, and so on. The titles were as endless as the *For Dummies* book series. Twenty years ago, the word "suck" was as offensive and risqué as the recently released title *Go the F**k to Sleep* is today. It was a publisher's marketing dream.

We had over fifteen agencies interested in the book and one that wanted an exclusive. We were elated but we didn't write it. Although we had some talent, we had no understanding of how hard it was to complete a book. We had never honed or practiced our writing skills. At the time, we lived in two different countries and the Internet was in its infancy; we didn't have any material, and we lacked job experience. We didn't just suck at finding jobs, we also sucked at writing a book.

We swallowed our dream. We soothed our egos with the understanding that there was still time; we were young. We tucked our incomplete manuscript away, and to this day it rests quietly in a filing cabinet in my basement.

Currently I am the co-owner of an events company with my husband, but the work has never been what I envisioned myself doing. For the last ten years it has been a career place-holder while my young children have needed my attention. When I think about the next stage of my career, I want it to be something I can be passionate about for the long haul and not just a place-holder.

Taking the time to build a new career held a lot of appeal, but it also meant struggling through the starting phase of a new venture. The long-term gains could be outstanding but the short-term pain might be more than I could bear, given the shaky economy and the immediate financial needs of our family. If I chose the career slice, I would be making a commitment to the future and to myself, but I would be making an immediate financial sacrifice to get things off the ground.

Three slices, one choice. I needed to pick the one that would make me feel like it was worth every bit of effort required to make it successful. I needed to believe that my choice would make me feel insanely, euphorically happy.

This is a lot to ask from a slice of pie.

Downward Dog Pie

I was standing in my kitchen debating the slice choice when Hillary, my personal assistant, interrupted my thoughts.

"Why do some women parade around the change room naked, with every hairy, saggy bit hanging out? Why can't they put on a towel or a muu-muu or something? It's gross." She wrinkled her nose as she asked me this question. Hillary is so stunningly beautiful that when I hired her, I told her in no uncertain terms that she would be fired if she didn't wear baggy, ill-fitting clothes or a burlap sack while she worked at my house.

Hillary's question caught me off guard, so I asked, "What change room are you talking about?"

"At yoga—hot yoga."

We both attended the same yoga studio. The changing rooms are styled in Zen-like fashion to complement the yoga experience.

"Maybe they're naked because they are just hot—like sweating hot, not sexy hot." I attempted an explanation.

"Oh, they're not hot, that's for sure. They stand there completely exposed while they roll up their yoga mat and sweat pours down their body like it's on a fat roller coaster. I just don't get it. I can't imagine why they would want everyone to look at them."

I winced as I listened. It felt like I physically shrank to become less visible. I was afraid to even imagine what Hillary saw when she looked at me. I reached under my hair and lifted it a bit; it felt thin and tired in my fingers.

"Oh, honey, I don't believe these women are thinking that everyone *wants* to look at them, I think they believe that *no one* is looking at them."

"What do you mean? They're naked, taking up half the space between the bench and the towel hooks while they wait to get in the shower. How can you say no one can see them? They're right there, all pasty, sweaty, and vagina-y."

Beautiful and nineteen—I remembered what that was like. I wasn't gorgeous at nineteen, but I had a firm body and would never have been caught dead hanging around naked in a change room. If I thought back hard enough, I could relate to Hillary's rant against the tide of exposed middle-aged women heading to the showers.

I breathed an audible sigh. "I think when you get to a certain age and you've had a couple of babies, suffered through a few dozen Pap tests, and squashed your breasts in a machine that flattens them like a thin piece of paper, standing around naked after hot yoga doesn't feel so embarrassing. I think it feels less like no one is looking and more like no cares, including yourself."

"I guess, but how hard is it to wrap yourself in a towel? Maybe the towels are too small?"

"Hmm. Yeah, maybe."

I stood there for a moment, lost. Hillary's words reminded me of the exact time I realized no one was looking at me anymore. It was a few years ago; I was waiting for a contractor to arrive at my house to fix a problem. He arrived early, and I hadn't had a chance to change out of my sweats.

"Hi. Are you lot forty-six?" He was young, tanned, and rugged looking. I looked at him while he stared at the work order on his clipboard.

"Yes. Lot forty-six."

"So, what do you need fixed?" His eyes looked past me into the hall. I felt the words stall in my mouth as I realized he saw me as a person who would sign the invoice and maybe offer him a coffee. I was nothing more than lot number forty-six. To him I wasn't a pretty young woman; I was a mom, a wife, an "excuse me, ma'am." The realization was shocking in a slow-motion way that made my stomach hurt. I had been officially cut off from my youth, from my optimistic, boundless soul that had carried me through so many of life's experiences. It was unnerving. It was horrible. It was the day I woke up and realized part of me had died: the young, pretty part.

"Heather? Do you want me to file these or do you want to go over them first?" Hillary's words brought me back to the moment.

"No, I'm okay. I mean, that's okay. Just file them. Thanks."

I didn't say any more as she sorted and categorized the invoices at my kitchen table. Working from home with three kids and a growing business, I depend on Hillary to be my personal lifesaver. Twenty years separate us, and every day I use some reference that she's never heard of—the converter, Ronald Reagan, and once, the infamous lip-syncing duo Milli Vanilli. When I asked if she knew about them, Hillary blinked and said, Oh, *I'm not hungry, thanks,* like they were type of cracker.

When she stands in my kitchen, Hillary is a living time machine. She is the point A to my point B. She is the before and I am the after. She is a mirror reflecting where I was twenty years ago. Some days this is okay, because it feels good *not* to be nineteen and teetering on emotional or fiscal disaster at the loss of a boyfriend or a job. But other days it's not okay. Until she shows up, it feels like it was just yesterday that I had limitless options, that I was young, beautiful, and believed there was nothing out of my reach.

When I was nineteen, I never thought I would be forty. I never dreamed I could stand naked in a changing room and not care who looked. What I couldn't see when I was young was that my middle-aged body and my sneaking grey hairs would represent the years marked by marriage, kids, career highs, and lost opportunities, that each line and wrinkle would mark time like lines across a calendar. Never for a moment did I think that standing in the raw with my sagging fleshy-bits out for all to see, I would feel okay with it—maybe even happy.

It was there in my kitchen that I chose my slice. Amongst the chaos of event folders and piles of racer swag surrounding me, I felt a calm that often precedes a large life decision. It came down to knowing what I was okay with in my life and knowing what I wasn't okay with. Keeping active and eating healthy are very important to me but I didn't need to be the fittest or the leanest person in the room; I was okay with my health slice. Having extra money undoubtedly would make my life easier but there was enough to get by; I was okay with my wealth slice.

I wasn't okay with my career slice. For so many years, I had tucked away the career slice like it was a special dream that I would only think about when everything else was going well - I knew that if I didn't take this chance now, I might never take it. Choosing the career slice, making a commitment to helping people through my writing, speaking, and training programs would fill this slice to bursting with happiness – I was sure of it.

One of the many races we created for Hark Events Inc.
The Emergency Services Adventure Race 2009, race start.

CHAPTER FIVE

* * *

Career: Lean In or Lie Down?

Q. How many motivational speakers does it take to change a light bulb?

A. None. Motivational speakers don't do anything, they just tell you how to find it within yourself to make a change.

My slice! I picked my slice. Reinventing myself is going to be awesome and fulfilling and amazing and holy crap, what was I thinking? I should have picked the health slice. I could have taken a few 'before' pictures and hopped on a stationary bike for a month. Or the wealth slice and dumped a bunch of loose change in a tin can and voila, emergency fund *done.* Heck, I could have even picked the community slice and cuddled kittens at the humane society. What was I doing? Picking the career slice meant thinking and digging and trying to understand who I was put on this earth to be. Attempting a do-over at forty is about as comfortable as wearing skinny jeans to a buffet. I just wanted to feel the happiness – the euphoria; I hadn't considered all the steps in between picking a slice and living the dream.

I needed a plan.

As I began creating an outline of my ideal career, I realized I had a bigger problem. I hadn't yet figured out who was going to pick up the slack in the family slice while I went searching for my work-bliss.

The Work-Life Imbalance

In June 2012 *The Atlantic* published an article penned by Anne-Marie Slaughter, "Why Women Still Can't Have It All."[4] The comment board blew up, with both women and men chiming in. Can you be a woman, have a stellar career, and still be a loving, attentive parent? Can you do both well and still be happy? Slaughter said no, and plenty of women said stop asking for so much, while others wondered how they could even compare their lives to Slaughter, a woman in the very top one percent of all earners. Men commented that this wasn't just a problem for women and that they also wished for greater balance between their work and family life.

I feel the term "work-life balance" is an oxymoron. Someone combined two functional words, "work" and "life," tossed in "balance," and created the definition for angst. There has never been a more challenging time for both men and women to define what it means to balance having both a career and a family. The fact that stereotypical lines have blurred for both sexes in recent history hasn't made the solution any clearer.

A recent survey claims that we are busiest at the age of thirty-three.[5] New research is saying that forty-four is the age at which we are the least happy. In that eleven-year span between thirty-three and forty-four, we are both busy and unhappy. Here I was attempting a career do-over in (statistically) the middle of the darkest decade. Was this the midlife blues, the middle-age spread, and the dreaded midlife crisis all rolled up into one? Being busy, tired, and overwhelmed between the ages of thirty-five and forty-five seems to be the norm according to both research and my own anecdotal evidenc. Prior to choosing this slice, my repeated attempts at managing both my work and family life to create harmony sent me on endless Google searches looking for answers.

In my quest, I found blogging guru Leo Babauta and his blog called 'Zen Habits.' He has over a million readers. He is an entrepreneur, a husband, and father to six children! He piqued my interest because his whole platform is about simplicity. I crave this type of existence. His posts are filled with ideas about finding balance and a sense of calm in our world filled with busy-ness. He openly and willingly shares his strategies for leading a simpler life. He has made dramatic changes to his slices, and he shares his failures and his triumphs with his readers. Many people ask him how he structures his day, and when I found a section on his website about his daily pattern, I thought maybe he was sharing the magic formula - the answer to the work life balance dilemma. As I read along, my eyebrows knit together and pinched my face. How was this schedule possible?

> 4:45 to 6 a.m.: Wake up, have coffee, read.
>
> 6 a.m.: Run (Mon, Wed, Fri and sometimes Saturday)
>
> 7-9 or 10 a.m.: Write, do other most important tasks.
>
> 10 a.m. to mid-afternoon: Smaller tasks, catch up on RSS feed reading, research various things I'm interested in (and will often blog about later). This really varies.
>
> Late afternoon–evening: Spend time with kids. Sometimes get a gym workout in. Or read. Also varies from day to day.
>
> Evening until 10 or 10:30 p.m.: Eat dinner, spend some time with wife and kids.[6]

I laughed out loud, because nowhere on this list was "do laundry," "get groceries," or "prep dinner." I didn't doubt his success or the path he chose to get there, but I wondered, who manages their six kids? Who makes sure that Zen daddy has quiet time for his mindful meditation? As I dug deeper in his posts, I found he gives due credit to his wife Eva. He praises her talents and dedication to managing their household and homeschooling their kids. They are partners in life together and while he is focused on the career slice, she is clearly the CEO of their family slice.

I'm not judging Leo's success or his personal choices on how they manage their household, but this wasn't going to work for me. I needed to find an answer to the question of what happens when Mommy is also a business builder? How can women attain this same level of career success *and* be Super-Zen-Mommy?

There are hundreds of ideas on how to achieve this potential harmony and I tried lots of them: make short lists, block out time, get rid of stuff, don't over-schedule, just say no, cook on Sundays, prepare all things the night before, don't press the snooze button, eat more protein. All of them were nice ideas, and some of them helpful, but none of them showed me how to bend the space-time continuum so that I could be in two places at once. None of them were solutions, just stop-gap measures that gave me a sense of control but didn't make me any less fatigued or that much happier.

The question remains: Is the work-life balance objectively impossible, or just impossible between the ages of thirty-five and forty-five? Is this simply a time when competing forces culminate at an inevitable apex called mid-life?

What if the answer was as simple as continuing with the status quo of busy and unhappy until things got better? Solve the problem by doing nothing. This sounds like a crappy solution for a self-help book but if you are unwilling or unable to make changes to affect a better outcome, and all your attempts lead to a no-win solution, then this period of fatigue and stress may just be part of the journey.

When our children were young and we were struggling with financial pressures, sleep deprivation, and the profound effect raising a family had on our freedom, adding a desire for career growth felt oppressive. It felt like too much to handle. The passive solution to wait out the storm, to get past the hardest days of managing work while being sleep-deprived and baby-weary, doesn't seem like a "Go get em" attitude, but it kept me from slipping into a place in which it felt like there was no end in sight. I found that taking a deep breath and knowing that "this too shall pass" was the most amicable answer for me.

While, "Just hang in there" is a cliché, it's reasonable to think we become less tired and less unhappy simply because our kids get older, our aging parents pass on, and it no longer matters what we look like in a bathing suit. Surviving this decade-long grind might be as simple as waiting out the storm.

I don't believe you can have work-life balance without sacrifice, and finding ways to maintain the juggling act without becoming resentful is a challenge. Everyday regular women are taking on this task of balancing these two desires; they are pursuing their goals, opening businesses, writing books, adventuring to foreign lands, and learning new languages - all the while nurturing their children and spouses or caring for aging parents - but it hasn't come without a trade-off.

Maybe there is a silver lining to this time of struggle. Perhaps in this decade, when we are the busiest and the least happy, we are offered a chance to ask the question, "What is most important to me?"

Chick-Pie

In my naiveté prior to the birth of my children, the concept of having a career and a family presented itself as a matter of logistics: create a schedule, stay focused, and pursue making babies and making money with vigor. Having a baby wasn't going to keep me from surging ahead. I would just work around my pregnancy, and then I would have childcare for the rest of the time. Who was going to stop me from reaching my career pinnacle?

No one would physically stop me, but stereotypes and gender roles would put up a good fight.

Before marriage and children, pursuing my career was as simple as setting my goals and taking the necessary action steps. I wasn't concerned about the dilemma faced by women who wanted both a giant slice of career and a picture-perfect slice of family. I wanted to believe that I was different—harder working and more driven than the average woman. When my babies were born, I would be like Madonna, running around cone-breasted, half-naked, breaking down gender barriers and female stereotypes. I would show the world how to effectively manage a career and kids.

I wanted so badly to be the exception to the rule that ironically, I became the rule with no exception. I became an over-scheduled, sleep-deprived working mom, juggling all my life slices, wondering how I would ever get up the next morning and do it all over again. And again. Forever.

I love my kids, and I love to work. I cherish hugs and snuggles and family outings, and at the same time I love talking about business ventures, creating new material, and generating marketing ideas. I've spent countless long nights taking care of sick babies and even longer days figuring out how to get my work done and still be on time for school pick up. When I take on contract work, I long to be home, and when I am home, I long to be at work. This constant balancing act between being a good parent and good business owner was, and still is, trying and confusing. One of my clients recommended I read, *Lean In.*

Sheryl Sandberg's book *Lean In: Women, Work, and the Will to Lead* is a call to women to find the courage and strength to keep pushing for career advancement, even if they have started or want to start a family. She has created a movement around the term "lean in" which is asking women to keep pushing or leaning into their work, pressing for promotions, work equality, and advancement in the workplace while leaning out of carrying the greater load of domestic chores. Although the book is a call to action for women in big business corporate America, I fear it failed to talk to the millions of female entrepreneurs in the country. When Sandberg asks, "What would you do if you weren't afraid?" The answer I would offer and the answer millions of woman have already chosen is, "leave". Identity, remuneration, and job security are attractive qualities that make working within a corporate structure seem like a no-brainer, but the lack of promotion, flexible scheduling, and career advancement for many women is a heavy price to pay when they are being asked to choose between their family and their career desires. When you start your own business you have effectively rendered most of Sheryl Sandberg's lean-in suggestions moot points. She suggests speaking up at meetings, staying at the table and being part of the discussion process – I say, I own the table. She suggests working as hard as you can up to the point of starting a family – I say, running your own business leaves you no other choice.

I applaud Sandberg's dedication to fostering more communication between women and breaking down the barriers for women in the workplace but I knew the words "lean in" weren't meant for me. Our stories, and our circumstances are different and they will appeal to women in different ways. I am a hard working entrepreneur, a middle class mother of three that will never earn a billion dollars. This is not an excuse or apology for not being more successful than I am. I chose self-employment for a myriad of reasons: flexible scheduling, challenging work, and great income potential. One of the less obvious benefits was that there wasn't a gendered infrastructure imposing my path to success. I didn't have to worry about what men thought of my ideas or how I presented them; I only had to worry about what *people* thought of my presentations and services. Running my own business meant that my clients were people that liked what I had to offer, and being female didn't make a difference in how successful I could become.

Even if the lean-in philosophy didn't apply to my work life, Sandberg's leaning-out of domestic duties suggestion was something I could vote for. When I picked the career slice to focus on, I was ready to do whatever it took to be successful. What was surprising was that my greatest challenge didn't come from the struggle of restarting my career; it came from inside my home. It showed itself in the form of piles: piles of stuff, piles of laundry, and piles of dishes. I often felt the sting of tackling the prickly issues of who was going to manage our household, the kids' schedules and the day-to-day operations of our home life while I began the process of rebuilding my career.

I can't hold a candle to some women's home organization skills but whether I'm good at these chores or not, I am the person that does the bulk of domestic management in our house. I needed to find a solution that would work for us.

Sandberg recommends creating a cohesive support system with your spouse and family members. While this is a logical idea that seems reasonable for two adults in a relationship, it is loaded with emotional discourse. It means trying to change domestic patterns that have been the same for the last two thousand years. Overcoming gender roles that have been consciously and subconsciously implanted into our lives is like navigating through my toddler's bedroom at night, littered with Lego pieces and toy Hot Rods. The toys are like relationship land mines, and walking into a dark room leaves you blind to stepping on them and setting off a chain reaction that might leave one or both of you wounded for a long time. Explaining to your spouse that the time needed to buy groceries, do the laundry, and prepare all the cooking are consuming any ability you might have to be successful at your career still leaves the question—so who's going to do them? My husband already had his share of duties to manage, and when we sat down to talk about the situation we really didn't find a good solution. We needed either more time or more money – or both. Having more time to be with our kids would mean one of us working less and we needed both incomes to cover costs of housing and living expenses. Paying for extra help could be part of the solution but this would require more money in the budget. Finding this money would mean one of us working more. Time and money: two factors most people would like a little bit more of. This is where it becomes harder to swallow Sandberg's advice about sharing responsibilities.

When Sandberg says she and her husband made a commitment to eating dinner together with the kids at 5:30pm each day, I wondered who actually makes the dinner? Who buys the groceries? These are problems that can be solved with time and money but without the benefit of one or the other in our household, these questions become fighting words.

My husband and I have both been working for twenty years and we have been together for twelve of them –at this point in our relationship our domestic patterns have been well established. Before kids, my husband was responsible for his full time job, some groceries, indoor and outdoor maintenance, and all things electronic. I managed my own business, extended family schedule, our vacations, the accounting, and bills. I was mostly in charge of the laundry, food prep, and general cleaning. When we added three kids into the mix, I wasn't magically released from those responsibilities; I just added new ones to the ones I already owned. I found the number of tasks to be completed in a day, absurd. No matter how hard I tried to combine a bountiful career and a functional family slice of pie, I still couldn't find the physical energy or time to make it all happen—happily. I was afraid that if I leaned in any more, I might actually fall over.

Despite this, I liked Sandberg's message: women need to lean into their careers to create a path that allows them to feel fulfilled at work, and lean out at home to enjoy a more balanced family slice.[7] What her book didn't answer was how to do this effectively without a secret bucket of money or a Mommy clone.

Choosing my career slice came at the price of other slices; they weren't completely ignored just on hold. I had to give myself permission to let go of the internal and external expectations I had of what life should be like rather than what it was really like. And while *Lean In* is the latest buzz phrase for business women, I will counter it with, *Let It Go.* I will use the most eye-rolling Disney phrase in this decade to describe how to release any whole pie expectation you may have by saying, *Let it go.*

We solved our problem the same way people solve a lot of problems; through trial and error and with a million work-arounds. We shuffled schedules, we avoided events that would take extra time or cost extra money and we hoped that these short term adjustments would allow me the opportunity to generate enough income until we could afford more help. We did what most people do, we made it work with what we had.

CHAPTER SIX

* * *

It's all Kittens and Unicorns

If you've ever tried to renovate your house, a room, or even an old table, you wouldn't be shocked if I said it will take twice as long and cost twice as much as you anticipated. I believe the same can be said about revising one's career.

Want to write a book in a year? Anticipate it will take two years. Want to launch a new training studio? Give yourself a budget and then double it. Looking to dive into your career slice while you ease back on your family slice? Plan to sell half your children or buy a giant cardboard cutout of yourself to use as a stand-in while you answer e-mails, design logos, and chat with prospective clients.

Since my new career involved three different skills (training, writing, and speaking), I treated them separately at first. I looked at each one as its own brand so that I could market them differently. The book became The Slice brand. My personal training business became Heather's Gym and my speaking engagements were marketed under my name.

The Book

Writing a book has been the single hardest thing I have done in my life to date. My degree in biochemistry was easier, finding a husband was easier, and natural childbirth was both easier and significantly faster.

I started with a book coach. I did it this way because even though I was capable of writing an eight hundred-word witty blog post, I couldn't write a cohesive eighty thousand-word book without a lot of help. Having a book coach was like getting an accelerated writing education and all it took to get started was an online intake form and my VISA number. Yes, sometimes it costs money to update your skills. Through my coach, I learned how to structure a book, edit my thoughts, and how to move a story along. I knew it would be worth the investment when The Ellen DeGeneres Show would call and say, "I love *Happy*! But Heather tell me, why just a slice?"

Writing a book reminds me of trying to lose weight; substitute calorie counts for word counts and it feels very similar. In the beginning it's easy to stick to the program because your determination is unwavering. The words fall onto the page like pounds dropping from your body. But like losing weight, somewhere in the middle of the process you hit a plateau – it gets harder, it's not as much fun, and you wonder if you'll ever get to your goal.

I wrote this book at night because this was the only time I could sit quietly without interruption. I'd start writing at 9:30pm and finish at 12:30am. I would try to write one thousand unedited words at a sitting. If I could write three days a week it would only take twenty-six weeks to complete the rough draft. Seven months to a finished first draft: no problem. I could've done it too, if I didn't have to also eat, parent, work, file taxes, or sleep.

Writing had to become a priority. To get it done, I gave up evenings with my husband and family. I sacrificed sleep and I accepted that I would be a zombie for the morning routine. While there were lots of things that suffered, there were big parts of the project that made me very happy. I gained an incredible sense of excitement from starting a goal I'd been dreaming about for twenty years. I gained an overwhelming amount of new information about writing and publishing books and I found an unknown appreciation for what it meant to be committed to the craft of writing.

And then it happened. People started asking, "So, how's your book coming?" The first few times it was kind of nice. The interest was pleasing in a way that made me feel good about myself. I would eagerly explain where I was in my page count and how it was coming along but as the months ticked by and thousands of words were written and rewritten, I began hoping that no one would ask. I stopped posting Facebook updates on my book progress because those four words, "How's your book coming?" might as well have been, "Are you still writing?" "Aren't you finished yet?" or "Hey! My uncle's cat just finished writing a book with its tail. When's your book going to be finished?"

It was the one question that could render me speechless. The moment I heard the words, I would feel a flash of intense pleasure and then the next instant I would feel creeping dread. I would rather get tasered than deliver a concise answer to why I hadn't yet finished this book. Well-meaning friends and family would ask with genuine interest in hearing when it would be ready for purchase, or when they might see it in a bookstore. No one knew that this question would induce mountains of self-loathing for a project that I felt would never end. How could they? The question, "So, how's your book coming?" ironically left me without words to answer.

Writing is supposed to be a wonderful, cathartic experience in which you can express your thoughts and creativity freely. The decision to share your words, however, can change that experience into a roller coaster ride of emotional and financial torment. If you've ever thought about writing a book, I've created a brief outline to prepare you for this stomach roiling, sweaty, long ride.

Creative Types are Often Alcoholics – I Get It

Step one: Start with an idea. An idea that other people might find enjoyable, relatable, or mysterious enough that they would be willing to spend a few dollars to know more. But don't pick something that has been done or overdone. The advice I was given was, don't write a memoir, and don't write a self-help book and absolutely, don't write a self-help memoir. If somehow I'd been able to harness the static electricity created from petting kittens to bring power to under privileged countries, I could have written that memoir, but

I didn't because this hasn't happened to me. So, I wrote about my marriage, and my children and how I eat cookies by the row that has nothing to do with triumphant journeys of self discovery and everything to do with finding one tiny way to be happier. My advice to you is: write about what you know. If it moves you enough to put it on paper, then that might be all that matters.

Step two: Have a nice glass of wine while you attempt to pick a title. This could take months or even years. The titles I started with came form this list: *Sigh; Forty is the New Tired; My Thighs are Touching; The UnSecret;* and at least five different arrangements of *Writing a Book is a Stupid Idea.*

Step three: Write a 70, 000 word first draft that no one will see because it is truly unreadable. Share parts of this draft with friends who don't really understand the shitty first draft concept and then wish you hadn't. Review this draft for continuity, tone, and overall structure. Pay someone to point out major flaws in your reasoning that you hadn't even considered. Take a peek at your calendar and then drink bottle of wine when you realize you have officially been writing your book for a year and it's nowhere near completion. Throw your shitty first draft in a pile for two months while you ruminate all the ego-crushing, red-pen marking the first edit produced.

Step four: Return to your manuscript. Open the book carefully like it's the Ark of the Covenant that might blind you with God's anger for your writing incompetence. Shield your eyes and inject Botox in your forehead as you reread the opening paragraph and try not to frown so hard your eyebrows touch your lips.

Take a deep breath and start to read it over. Then smile just a little when you find there are sections that aren't too bad. Drink some coffee and with renewed spirit, start working on the revisions.

Rewrite 69,000 of those first 70,000 words and feel pretty good about it.

Send it off to be edited and critiqued by a paid editor. Take antacids to fortify your stomach lining while you wait for the next set of comments and grammatical changes. Begin the new set of revisions with lots of coffee and an expanding waistline.

Send it to another editor for professional critiquing.

Have it returned with scathing hate edits. Drink. Throw the manuscript in the pile of "shit to do later."

Have one more person ask you, "How's the book coming?" and then quietly crawl away, stick your thumb in your mouth, and lay curled in the fetal position until you are in fact dead.

Eventually someone will bring you chocolate and a new glass of wine. You will laugh and then cry and then hopefully your anger will ramp up your desire. You might even turn your face upwards and yell to the heavens, "Did I murder someone in another lifetime? Are you punishing me by making me write a book?"

This is when you will vow with every bit of your soul, that you will finish this damn book even if it means your children will suffer scurvy from eating endless days of Spaghetti-os, your husband will sleep with your pillow so you will be forced to touch him when you finally get into bed, and your friends will wonder if you've abandoned them to live in a online world where Facebook 'likes' are your only means of connection. You commit to doing whatever it takes to answer the question "How's your book coming?" with the answer, "It's finished."

This is writing a book. This is writing a book when no one is paying you – it's a seemingly never ending task that you fit in and around all the other things you have to do. It's time consuming, it's costly and it's emotionally challenging. But when it's done – it's quite an accomplishment.

The Gym - Kittens, Unicorns, and Burpees

Losing weight, getting in shape, and eating healthy never go out of style. When I opened Heather's Gym, I knew exactly which clients *I wanted.* I wanted women that were tired of all the fitness noise, tired of trying to be thin and sometimes, just plain tired. I wanted to work with these women because I completely understood their frustration with trying to do it all and live up to an unrealistic body image. Heather's Gym became a place where people could define their own goals and start on a plan that would get them feeling better.

Fundamentally being healthy is one of the most important things you can do with your day but unless it's your job, it's not most people's "everything." I know this about my clients. They are busy, smart, fabulous people. When I first meet a client I spend a lot of time listening. I get their medical history, their exercise history, and most importantly I get to hear about what they are passionate about in life. My job as a trainer is to tap into each person's potential, and help find his or her spark. I look for the one thing that makes them who they are and this becomes the foundation for their program. You might think that I'm talking about a physical talent like strength or coordination, but a person's spark can come from anywhere. Some people are information hounds – they love learning, so I give them new information or techniques to digest every class. Other people have highly intense personalities – I use that intensity to their advantage whether it's a workout or starting a new eating plan. I find what people are good at and then I ask them to use that talent in their health slice. Once they see what they are capable of, they are more apt to own that ability. Each one of my clients tells me about their life goals – I help them get healthy on their way to those other dreams.

The fitness industry is fraught with fakes and instant fixes – I know how hard it is to achieve results, so when I had to come up with a logo for Heather's Gym, I balked at the usual symbols and Photoshopped images. I didn't want to use sculpted abs or a mountain peak because it all seemed so cliché. I picked a logo that poked fun at the fitness industry. I have a pink and purple color scheme with a unicorn in front of a rainbow surrounded by magical starbursts. My tagline is, *Making Your Fitness Dreams Come True.* Below my Disney-esque imagery are the words, 'Pretty Strong.' Whether people know I am mocking the industry or not, I believe the pursuit of the *image* of fitness has gotten out of hand. Fitness is about feeding your body, mind, and soul, habits that will become a lifestyle. Some days your kids will come before your workout, or your career will be forefront in your mind, and while excellent health is vital to enjoying life, I don't believe there's only one way or program to achieve that feeling. When people come to me to work on their health slice, I help them get results that are compatible with their lifestyle and dedication. I don't judge, I just listen and watch for the spark that will move them one bit forward in their quest.

Cue the fireworks.

The Talk - No Saucers Please

I have been speaking publicly long enough to know that having coffee available to your audience is an excellent addition to a seminar, but having coffee with saucers is not. Worse than pinging, vibrating cell phones is the constant click-clack of a thousand coffee cups being repeatedly placed on the saucer while a speaker you've paid to hear is revealing the "million dollar secret."

I use this one rule when I am preparing a presentation: Be informative and be entertaining in some combination, at every speech. When I first started presenting seminars, I couldn't quite figure out why some of my speeches went so well while others fell flat. As I practiced more I realized good speakers get paid a lot of money because they can engage an audience by capturing their emotional brain as well as their intellectual brain. Happy brains make a happy audience. Even when I felt I was both entertaining and informative, there were talks that I couldn't wait to finish and I'm sure the audience felt the same way. In fact, one of my worst moments on stage happened in my twenties. I cut my speech short by about thirty minutes and wrapped it up with one sentence, "Remember, your health is important, and enjoy the rest of the show." It was all crickets and saucers. When I analyzed the talk and all the things I did to prepare for it, I didn't take into consideration one vital element: I didn't know my audience. The talk was at a large trade show venue, the demographic was far older and there was a distracted atmosphere due to the open surroundings. My talk was targeted at younger, type -A personalities. The message and the humor were misplaced in the environment. Now when I prepare for a seminar, I start by asking, "Who is the audience?" I often go so far as to contact a percentage of them in advance, and then I tailor the information to be relevant for that group. A great speech tells a story that in some way links the speaker to the listener. All I need to find is the link we have in common and then apply the information in an entertaining way.

Motivational speaking, the final part of my career renovation, will be about bringing the concepts of Heather's Gym and *A Slice of Happy* to more people through seminars and training days. I've started speaking again and I'm gradually letting people know that I am available for their upcoming conferences or small gatherings. I get the most requests for my seminars titled: *Fat Got Your Tongue? Average With a Slice of Exceptional,* and of course, *A Slice of Happy – Because the Whole Pie is Overrated.*

My Secret Weapon

I'm often asked, "How can you really focus on one slice when there are so many competing things to do in the day?" I accomplish all of these tasks by using one technique. It is my secret weapon that helps me manage my work tasks and allows me extra time to spend with my husband and children. Wait, I just started laughing out loud. That's a big fat lie. A secret weapon that makes everything easier? What a cruel hoax– even I'd like it to be true.

I don't have a special technique or time management system that works. The truth is, most of the time lots of things don't get done. The laundry sits in piles to be folded, my upstairs always looks like we've been ransacked and I use my oven to store pans I haven't cleaned. I don't answer all my e-mails promptly, I have a million updates to be done on my websites, and I rarely write as much web content as I should to keep people interested. There's always a trade-off. You can't do it all.

While I have been working on this slice, I've stopped trying to have the perfect body, but I haven't stopped trying to be healthy. I've stopped trying to keep up with all of my kids' demands, but I haven't stopped loving and hugging them. I've stopped feeling guilty for not be available to be with my husband, but I haven't stopped enjoying the time we do have together. I've stopped worrying about trying to find perfection in all the slices. I've grabbed hold of this one and I'm giving it everything I have. Every day I wake up and swallow a big breath of perspective and then I do what I can.

Here's what it looks like. We use a family calendar that shows my husband's shift work schedule, my training sessions, the kids' events, as well as other special events. This calendar works about seventy percent of the time. The remaining thirty percent is the typical, "Oh-shit. I forgot." "Huh? I didn't notice that appointment there." And sometimes there seems to be a virtual time warp that sounds like, "Really – today is *that* day?" Focusing on my career doesn't mean that my schedule is free and clear, but it does mean that I make my work a priority over the hundred other things that happen in life. This would be the same no matter what slice you've chosen to work on.

In an attempt to help you in your own quest to pick a slice (or to give you material to complain about in your own book), I will post my average daily schedule. Please note: I don't always do this entire schedule myself. My husband is available for many pick-ups and some evening meals. His shift work is a monthly rotation where some weeks I am more alone and other weeks he is there to help a lot. My mother helps with the kids when I am teaching at night or have to do an event on the weekends when my husband is working. We use babysitters when they are available and each night we try to go over what is happening the next day.

7:15am Wake up.

7:15am-8:30am: Prep older kids for school.

8:30am-8:45am: Drop baby at daycare.

8:45am-9:00am: Clean kitchen.

9:00am-9:30am: Answer e-mails, catch up on paperwork, complete various to-do list items.

9:30am-2:30pm: Train clients.

2:30am-3:30am: Get groceries, do a load of laundry, work on business tasks.

3:30am-3:45am: Pick up older kids from school.

4:00pm-5:00pm: Prep dinner, talk to kids, schedule clients for next day.

5:00pm: Pick up baby from daycare.

5:00pm-6:00pm: Eat dinner with family. Prepare for evening boot camp classes.

6:00pm to 7:30pm: Boot camp.

7:30pm-9:00pm: Tidy kitchen, catch up with my husband, complete bedtime routine.

9:00pm-12:00am: Write, read, or prepare for seminars.

12:00am-5:00am: Be available for all children illnesses, bad dreams, and my own hormonally-induced insomnia.

5:00am-7:15am: Sleep like I'm in a coma and awake with disbelief that it's morning already.

Repeat.

Every day I feel a sense of excitement as I work on my career slice. I feel Hollywood happiness when I think about promoting this book. I feel engaged happiness when I am working with clients or creating seminar material and when my kids come home from school and my husband is there by my side, I feel heavenly happiness knowing that this new focus has made all my slices feel a little bit better.

A career is a calling. Our careers define us through the purpose and structure they provide. Ideally, we all want more than a job. We want to tap into the inherent talents, skills, and capabilities that lie within each of us, allowing ourselves to find more meaning in our work and lives. It seems some people are born knowing what they want to do, while others struggle to find work that gives them both a sense of accomplishment and an acceptable income. I found my calling, but it took time and a few missteps along the way.

I am a teacher who likes to tell a joke, a physical motivator with a message. Some days I am a personal trainer who takes people hiking or biking or has them perform a muscle dance with a kettle bell. Other days I'm a performer on stage, talking to hundreds of people and helping them find their slice of happiness.

All of these things make me feel like I'm living my passion. I'm going to continue to dive into this slice of pie and enjoy it for the first time in a long time. I am less afraid of failing and more concerned that I might run out of time. Finding a slice of career happiness can be a lot of trial and error, but when you find the right recipe, it tastes like the sweetest kind of success.

Logo Design for Heather's Gym.

PART III

The Slices

CHAPTER SEVEN

* * *

What's Your Slice?

I picked my slice, now it's your turn. Could you look at the slices - health, wealth, career, family, spirituality, community, leisure, and relationships and pick one that would make you happier? Is there one slice that would change your perspective if you allowed yourself the indulgence of diving in and getting started? Which one would you pick?

Would you finally get your health on track and live the lifestyle you've always wanted to? Would you head up a volunteer organization to protect a river in your neighborhood? Would you put every ounce of effort into reviving a failing relationship with a person you can't imagine living without? I picked the career slice, but the following chapters outline the slices I didn't pick, each filled with stories and adventures that might help you find happiness in your own slice.

Here's a list of the slices:

Sex, Lies and Leprechauns (the bonus) sex slice can be found on page 127.

Wait! Don't Sell That Kidney Yet, the wealth slice can be found on page145.

Charities and Other Things I Hate, the community slice can be found on 165.

Coffee for Breakfast and Wine for Dinner, the leisure slice can be found on page 179.

Death Sucks, the spiritualism slice can be found on page 200.

When you do pick your slice, give it its due presence. Enjoy it and savor it. Realize that while you are indulging in one piece of your pie, another one will be sliding to the background. Let it go. Enjoy your slice of happy—because the whole pie is overrated.

CHAPTER EIGHT: RELATIONSHIPS:

* * *

Relationships: Why More Marriages Don't End in Murder

My husband and I have been together for twelve years. We are on the leading edge of marriages in which traditional roles between a husband and wife have become blurred. My husband can efficiently change a baby's diaper in an airplane bathroom, cook a fantastic meal for eight, and choose an age appropriate gift for any birthday party. I'm equally good with a snow blower, the maintenance schedule of our cars and ensuring the taxes are filed on time—but it doesn't mean that we have it all figured out.

For any marriage that hopes to beat the separation statistics, there are only two words to consider: love and lust. Okay, just kidding. Those are great, but the real words that keep our marriage together are far less dramatic and contain way more syllables, they are: compromise and expectations. Staying married without murdering each other starts with the unromantic, unsexy, non-spontaneous discussion about what I want, what he wants, and what happens if we both fail.

*Relationship disclaimer: I believe everyone should be able to marry or love the person they choose in a healthy, mutually agreed upon union. My stories are dripping with stereotypical, heterosexual examples because that's the life I live. If you are in fact less stereotypical, I cheer for you and encourage you to change the pronouns to suit your personal situation.

The Worst Name You Can Call Your Spouse

"I need to have a talk with Cam," my girlfriend Margaret said.

"Uh-oh. What's up?" We were out for a run, both trying to get back in shape after many months of shapelessness. Margaret and Cam have been married for sixteen years.

"He thinks he's still twenty years old when it comes to sports, and he keeps injuring himself—which makes him miserable, and he morphs into an asshole."

"Ha! That's like the 'man cold,' but with a sprained ankle. A 'man-jury,'" I quipped.

"Exactly. It's crappy because when he's grumpy, it affects me and my happiness."

"I'm in the same place. I asked my husband to help me with a website project, and I'm disappointed with the results. If I don't say something in a sane, ego-smoothing way, it's going to come out like *I'm* crazy."

We continued our run in contemplative thought, each of us trying to understand the men in our lives and how best to stay married to them. Margaret glanced at me as we ran along the path. "The only serious talks I have with my husband are about disappointment. You know, having an expectation and then being deflated with the result of his efforts."

I nodded and added, "Yup, disappointment and growing up. Do they ever grow up?" We both laughed as we eased the pace.

Margaret dug deeper into the idea. "Do you think it's us? Could there be something wrong with us?"

"No. Okay, yes. We're never happy. When they do something for us, we're never satisfied."

As much as it pains me to admit, it seems I am *never* satisfied. If my husband buys groceries, I complain about the type of cheese he bought; if he takes the kids to the park, I complain that he brought them home hungry. I am never satisfied with what he actually does; I am angry because he doesn't do these things the way I do. I expect him to be me, and when he doesn't match up to my ability, I ask myself, *Isn't it okay to get a bit angry? Isn't it okay to expect more?* There are many days when I say nothing and just let things slide. There are other days when my mouth pops open before I can stop it. "We've been buying the same cheese for the last ten years—how can you not know we buy marble cheddar?" I'll say, or "Our kids eat food every day. This is not news. You can't just *forget* to feed them." And with a puzzled look, my husband will wonder why I'm acting this way. Is this one of *those* days? 'Those days' can be summed up as the days when I think it's obvious what's wrong with the scenario, and he thinks I'm overreacting and a little bit crazy—you know, *those* days.

When I question my husband's ability or his execution of a task, it germinates the seed of truth or the "little bit crazy" that makes my husband say, "See?" It's his way of encapsulating all the things I pick on, adding them up, and reaching a total that equals 'nag.' As a couple we are very careful to avoid using words that are hurtful, but after enough years of togetherness, some words don't need to be spoken because they can be sensed. Historically, my husband will leave the room before we start down the path of name calling, but it doesn't mean that the feelings aren't there.

For most women, the name we avoid, the name that strikes shame and anger in our sense of being, the name I don't even like to type because it comes with such a negative impact, is "bitch." The mere mention of being a bitch makes me recoil and look around in the hopes that no one is referring to me. When I point out something that I'm not happy about to my husband, I don't think I am being a bitch or a nag; I'm merely trying to understand why we aren't on the same page. It doesn't take many misunderstandings to sound like I'm nagging. The bitch label creeps up around me because to him it feels like my words are little hammers tapping away on his skull until I poke a hole through it. And while I think I'm communicating in an inoffensive way, my husband, feels like I can't stop pointing his failings out, and he can't begin to imagine what would ever make me happy. It's this misunderstanding—that I'm just trying to get something done, and he's just doing it the way he feels is best—that leads me down the slippery slope of stereotypical name calling. If I'm going to be called a nag, a ball and chain, or that pinnacle of offensiveness, a bitch, then I shamelessly retaliate with a fiery spirit, using my formidable tongue to cut to the core with my words.

I have found the one word that hits men the hardest, that makes a man want to drop his head like a wild bull in a ring and charge me like I'm a toreador, is "useless." Generally speaking, men like to fix things, solve things, and be useful. Reducing them to a word that means inert, unfixable, or good-for-nothing makes them feel bad. I know it doesn't even sound like a swear word, but calling men "useless" undermines their purpose, their sense of self, and their very reason for existing. The worst thing you can call your wife is a bitch, and the worst thing you can call your husband is useless (or useless asshole, if you feel it needs a swear word).

The problem is, none of this literal or figurative name calling gets either of us anywhere.

As Margaret and I finished jogging, we paused to stretch out our hamstrings on the picnic bench near the track. I thought about the last time my nagging persona made an appearance. "Last week my husband said he was going to drywall the garage, and he asked if I would help him hold the drywall while he nailed it in place. I said, 'Yes, honey, I will hold a thousand-pound wall of Sheetrock while you position it.' As he climbed the ladder, I said, 'Why didn't you cut this first? How come you're using a hammer instead of the compression nailer? Did you seal the insulation before you started? Why didn't you just ask the drywall guys to do it—wouldn't that have been easier?' Then he wanted to kill me. He wanted to drop the slab of drywall on my head to make me shut up. But I couldn't stop. My mouth had been taken over by a poltergeist that wanted my marriage to end in murder. Murder by renovation."

"But what if the way they're doing it, whatever they're doing, is just dumb?" Margaret asked the question that has confounded women forever.

"It doesn't matter, because we watch them and judge them for not doing it the way we wanted. They are useless, and we are bitches."

"But I spend so much effort trying not to be like that. I really do."

"I know," I empathized.

"I think I'm really good at not berating my husband."

"I'm sure you are, but they think they're awesome at everything and all we do is complain."

"Uh-huh. So what's the answer?" Margaret asked.

"I don't know—take separate vacations? Don't watch him assemble Ikea furniture? Don't offer to buy a birthday present for his mother? There is no answer, because if you want to stay married, you have to find a decent work-around for most things and save your sacred requests for times that are deal breakers."

"But this seems unfair."

"Marriages have confusing rules now," I sighed as I put on my hoodie. "None of this existed three hundred years ago. Men used to go off to war or on long trips—they would get on a horse and ride off and maybe come back in the spring. It gave us a chance to miss them. We ruled the home front. Now our roles get all mashed up together in a weird place of whose job it is to take out the garbage. Every shitty, unimportant task has become one more reason to be disappointed in each other."

"Hmm. I think I'll leave Cam's 'manjury' alone."

At the time of writing this, the divorce rate in America for a first marriage is 41 percent, for a second marriage 60 percent, and for a third marriage 73 percent.[8]

This is a staggering statistic. It makes me fearful for my own marriage. Our odds of staying together are only slightly better than fifty-fifty. I've watched so many friends separate and divorce that I wonder if it's inevitable. When I find out another couple has changed their Facebook status from married to single, I want to know why. Why did their marriage fail? How can I protect my family from the possibility of divorce? I'm not an advocate for staying in a relationship that is dangerous, miserable, or unfulfilling, but I want to believe that if I follow the secret relationship formula, I will be exempt from those outcomes. I want to be able to preserve this slice and enjoy it.

Mark and I are more similar in our likes and habits than we are different. We can sit in the car for hours and fill the time with great talks or comfortable silence. We prefer to be together when doing even mundane tasks than doing them apart. We share a love for good food, small get-togethers, and spending time in nature. When my husband proposed to me at the top of a mountain that we had biked up, I knew it was for the right reason. We both agreed that life was better together than apart. We felt like we could reach greater heights as a team than as individuals.

That's not to say we are without our share of problems. We argue about domestic chores, we regularly get annoyed by how much 'stuff' we have and often we (*I*) have resentment issues with whose turn it is to get out of the house with their respective friends. We argue about the E on the gas tank gauge and what is really meant by *empty*. We argue about wet towels, random socks, and the endless dishwasher duty. While we aren't big on the toll of these arguments, we are big on staying married. With this as the end goal, we came to an agreement two years into our marriage, on my birthday. It's one of the relationship pillars that has helped us from becoming a national divorce statistic.

The Agreement

My birthday is February 13, the day before Valentine's Day. This puts me in the category of people that suffer from present neglect around a Hallmark holiday. Mark was a shift-working police officer at the time and wasn't home when I came into the kitchen on the morning of my birthday. There was a large box on the counter. It wasn't wrapped, and it had an image of a coffeemaker on the front. As I walked up to it, I had a small smile on my face in anticipation of what might be inside. We'd been married for two years; we were still toting around love euphoria hormones. It was way too early in the honeymoon phase for an appliance gift so I looked forward to the surprise. There was a torn piece of paper taped to the top of the box. In faded red marker it read:

Happy Birthday

Mark.

I felt my heart sink. I didn't want to be disappointed, but I couldn't help the building tide of emotions coming forward. A rush of thoughts came to my mind.

He tore a piece of paper as a card and he signed it "Mark"? Not "Love, Mark" or with a heart by his name. Where was my name? "Honey," "Sweetie," or even just "Heather"? Is this box a giant disguise for a tiny piece of jewelry? Surely it can't be a coffeemaker. We have one already. There has to be more. Maybe he booked us a dinner reservation?

As I removed my "card," I realized that the box was sealed shut like it had come off the shelf at Walmart. It looked like it had come right from a store, because it had. It was a coffeemaker. It had an instruction manual and a plug.

Why would he buy me a coffeemaker? This was supposed to be a gift for me, not a gift for us. Was I supposed to make him coffee?

The phone rang.

"Hi. Happy birthday, babe." I could hear him smiling while he said this. "Did you get my present?"

"Yes. Thanks. I liked the card." My voice was flat.

"Oh, I'm sorry. I was in a rush to get to work."

"I know. My birthday just sneaks up. It's always so hard to know when it is, *even though it's on the same day every year.*"

"Wow. I thought you'd like it." His "wow" was an "I can't believe you are saying this" kind of wow.

"But I feel like you bought it for yourself. You're the one who doesn't like the coffeemaker we have, so you bought me one for *my* birthday?" As hard as I tried to be strong, a little tear escaped and there was a hiccup in my voice.

I cried because it was more than just the coffeemaker. We were practically newlyweds, and already I was on the receiving end of a hurried, unwrapped present that he picked up on a lunch break. He bought an appliance for the house, stuck a piece of paper on it, and hoped I would be happy. I was hurt that he didn't think about a gift that would be special to me. I was hurt because on his birthday I buy him man toys, with built-in secret compartments for carrying knives. I search out ideas that involve hunting, survival, destruction, or speed and the potential for injury. My birthday gift was not just a coffeemaker—to me it was a statement. All of my unspoken expectations about our relationship were wrapped up in this present. The coffeemaker made me feel like I wasn't important.

I could hear him take a deep breath, "No, sweetie, I bought the coffeemaker because it's one of *our* things. I love having coffee with you in the morning. There is no better way to start the day. When I saw it, it made me think about us being together doing something we enjoy. I didn't mean to hurt you—I love you."

To my husband, it was a thoughtful gift; to me, it might as well have been a vacuum. He thinks a five-star, all-inclusive vacation is boring, and I think tents, tarps, and food barrels should be packed only in the event of Armageddon. He says planning takes away the fun; I say spontaneity is for a single man with a condom in his wallet.

That's when we started managing our relationship expectations. Birthdays, anniversaries, vacations, in-law visits, major purchases—anything that could lead to the dissolution of our marriage, we manage by talking about our expectations before the event.

You don't have to draw circles in a catalogue or drop hints about your love of sparkly accessories. It's much better to be straightforward and speak to each other without code words. We keep it simple, yet specific. "I don't want flowers, but I would like to go out to dinner at my favorite restaurant." Then I actually name my favorite restaurant. We set up basic expectations. "If you remember my birthday within one week of the actual date, I won't buy you a piece of furniture for yours." It works for us, and we do it religiously in order to keep our marriage on track.

The Checklist

Marriage used to be a transaction: seven goats, two cows, fifty acres, and three blankets were enough to trade a woman into marriage. Thankfully, women have graduated from being property to being proprietors, and now we look for partners who fulfill many of our emotional and physical needs. We have a checklist as long as the gear list for an Everest expedition, and we strive to have it all—well, most of it.

Prior to marriage, conversations with my best friend often revolved around daydreaming the right man into existence. Recently, in a restaurant, I overheard two girlfriends chatting in the booth behind me. I could hear only one side of the conversation, from a young woman outlining what she wanted in a man. As Booth Girl sipped her iced tea, she waxed poetic about the kind of man that would be right for her.

"I don't know...I mean, I'd like a guy that's funny. Funny, thoughtful and strong. I think it's important to be strong but, you know, not a steroid muscle-freak but strong like a guy that takes a stand for something. And protective, like a guy that will make sure I'm okay but not beat up other guys because they look at me. Romance is important too—not a ton, but something nice on my birthday and Valentine's Day. I wouldn't expect romance all the time that would feel forced; sometimes I just want to have sex. So I guess I would have to say, good in bed. But not a huge penis. Huge penises are scary.

More like a nice size. And a provider, because I know I want to have kids, so if he has a decent job, that would help, and he would need to be good with the kids and caring and attentive. I guess what I want is a guy who's thoughtful but in an intuitive way, like he senses my needs without me telling him all the time what I want. Smart is important, so we can talk about things and the future and, you know, just making sure we have good, open communication. That's all."

When she was done talking, I mentally translated her fairy-tale dream prince with a moderate-sized penis and a plush bank account into the following:

> Dear Prince Charming,
>
> Please provide for me all the things in life that I need to be happy. It would be best if you were a sword-wielding, romantic hero who likes to openly express your feelings. You should be well skilled in satisfying my sexual desire and reading my mind on a daily basis. Tell me I'm beautiful, and keep telling me when I am old and wrinkled. Remember my birthday, and be able to dance or sing (every woman likes a man who can carry a tune or keep a beat). If you are unable to provide any of these characteristics, all can easily be overlooked if you are rich.
>
> Sincerely,
>
> Barbie Princess

That's it. The list was simple: be romantic, funny, charming, protective, sympathetic, strong, thoughtful, caring, sensitive, smart, intuitive, heroic, sexy, attractive, and a good provider with strong family values.

Sixteen things. This made me ponder what men want from women. I came up with four:

1. Sex
2. Attention
3. Praise
4. To be left alone when they don't want sex, attention, or praise.

They want four things. Have sex with them regularly. Pay attention when they are telling you why a certain size bolt is not going to work on that engine. Shower them with praise for completing the most mundane task of placing their coffee mug in the dishwasher, and leave them alone if you are not fulfilling one of the aforementioned three. It sounds like a stereotype because it is. No one enters a relationship with the intent of becoming a person that can be typified, but it happens.

Every day I fight off the encroaching stereotype I swore I'd never become: a harried, tired, unkempt, nagging wife that used to be an organized, refreshed, fit, understanding woman. And it's truly a fight to crawl my way out of that character. It's easy to stop taking care of myself when there are so many other pressing needs of a family or career. Most spouses are no different. Our potential mates start out with the desirable traits of being sexy, competent, and rugged, until our veil is lifted (literally) and we see a slightly grubby, inattentive, self-absorbed child in man-sized pants. If the euphoria of love hormones lasts for only about two years, why would anyone ever want to get or stay married?

Because hopefully, you didn't just fall in love with your partner, but somewhere along the line you fell in *like* with your spouse. It's the *like* that keeps you married. It's the *like* that helps you through the tough times. Same desires, different code words.

Men: praise, hero worship, and sex.

Women: compliments, goddess worship, and foot massages.

At the end of the day, both partners just want to be liked. Liking your spouse allows a marriage to survive a renovation, an extended in-law vacation, or protracted sleep deprivation. If you have chosen marriage, it is a commitment that needs attention, nurturing, and sometimes space. The relationship slice is still just that, a slice. It's best to keep that in mind when you are debating which relationship items need critical attention and which ones can be left alone. A long-term marriage falls far short of imitating a romantic movie story line, but what it lacks in lust and spontaneity it makes up for in a slow-simmering plot I call *like.*

But How Do You Know?

I dated the good guy, bad guy, wrong guy, almost right guy, sexy guy, successful guy, dumb guy, badass guy, and every combination of the above. I was looking for a man to make me happy. It took a long time to learn that I needed to know how to make myself happy, and then maybe I could add in a person to complement the bounty I had to offer. No one could own my happiness but me.

When I was ready for the right man, I had sorted out my core expectations and figured out my man formula. I had what I called the "test of three," an easy way to tell whether a date was even remotely viable as a life partner. The test of three was simple: dogs, waiters, kids. The triad. If a man could be nice to animals, then I believed he had a certain level of compassion. If a man could be nice to someone in the service industry, then to me it was a sign of respect. Finally, if a man was comfortable with the sticky, chubby fingers of a toddler, then he passed the toughest of the triad tests. A man who could hang out with children was a man who could show love.

As I sat in my kitchen reflecting on this, the phone rang.

"Hi, Mom."

"So, how's it going with Mark?"

"Good—he's nice. We went hiking. I brought the dog." We had been dating for a few weeks by this time.

"Did he like her?" My mom had seen many suitors fail my test of three. I'd recently turned thirty-one, and she hoped Mark would pass the boyfriend litmus test.

"Yes, he's practically a dog trainer. His brother has hunting dogs, and they grew up with them."

"Good. Then he passes the dog test?"

"Yes. He even talks to the dog like a baby. 'Awww, what a good widdle doggy.' He brought his camera too!"

"Really? A man that brings a camera, that's impressive." This was a time before cameras became confused with phones.

"I know! He took pictures of me with the dog."

"Are you sure this test of three works? You dated the last guy for a year, and he didn't pass any of them."

"Yes, Mom. That's why we broke up."

"But he had money. Why isn't that one of the three?"

"Mom, money isn't everything. Mark passed dogs and waiters. Now I just have to see if he likes kids."

The final test: kids. To this day my husband connects with kids on a level I will never understand. He is the dad that wrestles on the floor while he's being pummeled by little fists and loves every second of it. He's the first to pack the kids in the car and take them on every adventure imaginable including the hardware store, the ski hill, and the gym with the fun rings and heavy weights. Perhaps some people maintain a piece of their kid-ness and it's linked into their DNA? Either way I'm grateful his kid ability is unparalleled. My husband passed the test of three; he is compassionate, respectful, and loving. (Now if only I were a dog, waiter, or kid.)

I am practical about my marriage, and I am honest. We enjoy spending time together, we share common interests, and we both have activities that don't involve the other person. Along the way, we've made a few additions to our list of expectations that has helped keep us together through the inevitable ups and downs of our relationship.

Your Spouse Is Not Your Best Friend

Mark and I talk with disbelief about the fact that margarine is still considered a food. We talk about CrossFit and whether the Olympic lift referred to as 'snatch' should be included in workouts. We have long discussions about minimizing the stuff in our lives. We talk about helping our kids find their passions, and we share our own dreams and ambitions. We tell each other jokes, compare our days, and embrace technology for quick personal updates through texts and photos.

But my husband is not my BFF.

I know. It sounds wrong.

Contrary to what you may have read or heard in blogs and love songs, the person you marry should not share the title of spouse and best friend. This goes against every bit of Disney wisdom and self-help relationship guide rhetoric. I've heard it said countless times: "My husband or wife is my best friend." It makes me pause. People get married because they fall in love, they complement each other, they trust each other, and they are good together. People get married because they want to build a life with each other, have children, and maybe own a house. Ultimately they are together because they have common goals, common enemies, or shared interests. This may sound exactly like having a best friend, but here's the difference: you can tell your best friend things that you wouldn't and shouldn't tell your life partner. Not every thought that crosses your mind should be shared with your spouse. You might think this is common sense, but somewhere in the relationship guidebooks the word "communication" became confused with the word "confession." Making confessions to your spouse does not make either of you happier. Telling your better half that you don't like his hair, saying you wish she wouldn't breathe the way she does, or explaining in detail your alone time in the bathroom is too much information. These are confessions.

Confessions result in one of two outcomes. If you point out a personal trait that isn't to your liking (such as bad hair, love handles, or ass dimples), you make your partner feel bad about himself or herself. If you give too much information about yourself (I'm a nervous driver, I eat when I'm upset, I don't like meeting new people), over time your partner quietly judges you—and then eventually you feel bad about yourself. Remember, I am talking about living with the same person for twenty years or more. All of these negative confessions, like "I hate my thighs," "I'm so disorganized," or "Why can't I get a promotion?" add up and, at some point, tip the scale against being married. Negatively poking your own self-esteem or constantly trying to 'fix' your partner's problems acts like water wearing away a breakwater. Over time the constant friction erodes the very reason you got together in the first place. If you like the institution of marriage and would like to stay married, find a way to stop confiding in your spouse about things that are irrelevant to the success of your relationship.

Note: Confessions are not the same as compromises.

Compromises are an absolutely necessary part of marriage, but confessions can lead to the breakdown of your loving partnership. If something is not working in your relationship, then you need to communicate to find a compromise. But blathering tell-alls should be saved for a whine fest with the girls or a phone chat with your BFF.

My Confession

My husband is a hottie. I see women ogle him at the beach, at parties, and even at the grocery store. It makes me feel insecure. I've taken a vow of silence that keeps me from going on about my physical attributes I loathe. I just don't do it.

"Hey, Tina, do you have a cosmetic surgery wish list?"

"Doesn't everyone?" She laughed as if I'd asked a rhetorical question.

"It's crazy, but as I've gotten older, my list has changed. It used to be about a smaller nose and bigger boobs, and now it's all about my face and neck." I pulled the corner of my eye toward my hairline and sighed.

"I'm always telling my husband I want never-ending, lifetime hair removal—arms, legs, lip." Tina is half Italian and has the most gorgeous, model-thick hair. It cascades down to her shoulders with a natural soft curl, and when she talks about blow-drying it, she says it's an all-day process. She has also told me that with her mane of hair comes all the other "extra" hair.

"Hang on. You talk to your husband about your surgical wish list?" I asked.

"Of course. We talk about what we'd get done and laugh at each other."

"Wow." I was truly shocked, and I paused before telling her my confession. "I never say anything to my husband about what I hate. Never. I don't talk about my fat roll, the bump on my nose, or the addition of a new chin after our three babies. I don't mention the wrinkles on my forehead, and I never talk about my boobs."

"Why? You're usually so open. I figured you've told him how you want an investment fund to save for your face lift in ten years."

"Bah! No. That's my secret fund. If I talk about all these shitty things to my husband, it's only a matter of time before he wonders why I don't do anything about them. He's six years younger than I am."

"Right, I forgot."

"Exactly. You forgot because I never mention it. Maybe he will forget that I am older and more wrinkled because I never talk about it. See?"

"You're crazy."

"No, I'm prepared. I'm making sure that my own whining doesn't backfire and produce the exact result I don't want. Now take my advice and don't talk about your faults; no guy wants to listen to you complain. Just like we don't want to watch them play video games. Just tell him about the good stuff, like how your beautiful eyes got mistaken for emeralds at the jewelers and how someone slipped you a card to become a hair model at lunch the other day."

That's how I stay confident about my marriage to my overly sexy husband. When I need to bemoan my ass fat, I simply call my best friend. She will neither care nor suggest ways that I could fix it. She will let me complain and whine, and she will listen while I talk and eat ice cream.

You can tell your best friend that you are mad at your husband, and she will tell you to relax. Say the same thing to your husband, and he will mentally say, *What else is new?* Tell your BFF you feel fat, and she will hush you and hug you through the phone. Tell your husband, and he will suggest ways you could improve your eating habits. Tell your best friend that you would love to just get away from it all, and she will sigh and dream with you about an all-inclusive vacation in heaven. Say the same words to your husband, and he will say, "Sure, go ahead, but make sure the house is organized, the schedule laid out, and the groceries are stocked and leave everything labeled, and color coded." Okay, he doesn't actually say that, but it's implied when he calls within fifteen minutes of my departure, wondering where his pants are.

Best friends are best friends. Marriages are marriages. Don't mistake the two and feel confused about your spouse's commitment to you just because he or she doesn't support your every thought. Women: your husband is not your BFF. Men: your wife is not your mother. Ladies: stop talking to your husbands about your period. Men: stop asking what's for dinner and being confused when it's time to pack the kid's lunches. Friends are like angels, and mothers are like saints. Neither you nor your spouse is an angel or a saint to each other, so lower the bar and enjoy your partnership for what it *can* give you.

What is the formula? Is there a way to ensure your marriage lasts? For every relationship problem, there are dozens of experts willing to give you an answer or solution that worked for them: *Women Who Love Too Much, The Five Love Languages, Relationship Rescue,* and so on. With so much advice out there, I ask myself: What would make my marriage simpler? Can't I just use common sense to sort out the problems? That approach would make the relationship equation look like a piece of cake (or pie), but it doesn't appear to work that way. Relationships are like a complex math equation calculated with emotional algebra. They are a balancing act equivalent to performances by the tightrope gymnasts of *Cirque du Soleil.* Somewhere amongst all the roles you each play and the variables in your life, there is still a "you," a singular person with your own needs and desires. *You* are still a person separate from your marriage, separate from the expectations, the negotiations that you and your partner perform to stay together.

The common sense answer is balance. Each partner needs a bit of group therapy offered up on annual fishing trips or girls-only weekends, as well as some alone time to pursue his or her own hobbies. If these excursions aren't on your list, then I suggest you find one friend who will listen to your confessions and help you when you need to drop the rosy-relationship façade. All relationships need support, and having a friend to voice rational and irrational complaints to, someone other than your spouse, is a good way to diffuse some of your complaints and confessions and help you keep the happiness in your marriage.

No marriage is perfect, but is it worth it? In my opinion, yes. If marriage is part of *your* long-term plan, with common goals and a desire for family, then the ups and downs are part of the package. Without a doubt, a successful marriage takes work. It requires that each partner enter the union with a full understanding of the requirements of the position. Ultimately, the effort you put in will be equal to the result that you get out. The need to be liked is universal, and if marriage can fulfill that need on a regular basis, then you deserve to enjoy this slice to its fullest.

Compromise

I am guilty of crushing my husband's dreams. I think we all are capable of doing that to our spouses from time to time. My husband will come home excited about a business venture or a special vacation, and when I hear him talk about it, I allow a dream-crushing pause before responding, "Oh, have you really thought about this? Do you think this is a good idea right now?" He may agree with my assessment or disagree, but either way, I have crushed his dream like a crunchy bug under the giant shoe I call 'living responsibly.' I've crushed lots of them. Living on a big piece of land with acreage. Owning a motorcycle. Opening a hunting camp in rural anywhere. Living off the grid. A work stint in Bosnia as a uniformed officer to help a country in civil war. I've squashed, ignored, and waved away so many of his dreams that ten years into our marriage, I had to stop. I had to stop expecting my husband to continually give up his fantasies in order to be boring, more responsible, and well, like me.

Now that we have a family, there is a stereotypical assumption that we own a minivan, but we don't. Without a doubt we *should* be the owners of a family box with wheels and drop-down entertainment centers, a land-cruising rectangle with double auto-open side doors and extra-wide coffee holders to contain our mega insulated caffeine carafes—but we aren't. I swore I would never succumb to owning one of these asexual means of transport, but something changed - we had three kids. Now I fantasize about having an easy-to-load, reliable vehicle to move people and gear in a way that is simple and time-efficient. Currently we own an eight-year-old Nissan SUV and an eleven-year-old VW Jetta. We jam in three car seats, and getting them buckled is like bathing a cat. I salivate when my friends roll up in a Dodge Caravan, fully loaded with dual climate control centers and mini-televisions that would make my kids catatonic for long drives.

But.

My husband has a different dream.

My husband enjoys hunting, fishing, and rugby and has almost no interest in cars, except one, and it's not a car, it's a truck: the Land Rover 110 Defender. The name will mean nothing to you unless your spouse belongs to this odd club or you have a thing for trucks that look like they came out of a comic book. If you happen to be a 110 Defender virgin, I will try to enlighten you on the mystique of this machine. The name screams rogue, rugged survivalist, exploring and protecting the earth while remaining sexy and cool. The truck's look and design haven't changed in forty-two years, the more rugged and combat-ready, the more appealing. When he showed me his fantasy all-terrain vehicle for the first time, I said, "It's a bit narrow. It looks like it would tip over."

He rolled his eyes and turned away as he said, "It's narrow so it can travel on a goat path at the edge of a mountain." He didn't add "*stupid*," but I'm pretty sure it was implied.

The Land Rover 110 Defender is my husband's porn. Well, the *other* porn. For some reason unknown to me, these trucks are not available for import from the UK until they are twenty-five years old. This means his Defender was made sometime in the 1980s. The only thing I have from the '80s is an old passport complete with feathered hair photo.

Mark has been looking at these trucks for the better part of ten years. He would surf the "special imports" section on the Internet and announce to me when a new truck listing was uploaded.

He yelled downstairs to me, "Hey honey, come and see this truck." I feigned interest as I thought about sitting at my computer to search for a new house. We had recently sold our first house while the market was favorable, but we hadn't yet found somewhere to live. I spent hours on multiple listing services searching for the right place. If there was an *other* porn for women, it would be online real estate. As I searched prices and floor plans, I found a house that I wanted.

I was so excited I yelled upstairs to Mark, "Come see this house! I want to buy *this* house," I said, showing Mark the website with the model home and the dotted lines of our demarcated rooms. He glanced at it, and suddenly he seemed to crouch a bit, his eyes narrowed, and he cocked his head to the side. He sniffed the air and licked his lips like he was hunting prey. I was confused. I thought he might be going into a man coma because I was talking, but then at lightning speed, he pounced.

"Okay, you get that house, I get a Land Rover. Deal?" His primal brain stem sensed a weakening in my "common sense" defenses against this attack.

"Whoa. Don't you want to see the house?"

"No."

My husband hates sales and negotiating. He was closing the deal and effectively eliminating all objections by simple sweeping his hand across the house package and saying, "You get aaaall this. And I get a truck."

I knew he was serious and I knew I had about five seconds to compute the real cost of the truck. Would we have enough money for both my dream home and his 'mantasy?' Would this be a good compromise? No mini-van, in exchange for a LandRover for him and my dream home for me. I tried to think about the variable costs of having an extra vehicle. There was the base price, plus the transfer taxes, repair and upkeep, additional insurance, and gas. Then there were the intangible costs, like taking the truck for a quick spin through the mud, getting stuck, calling a friend with another truck to get out of the mud, and drinking beer while discussing the mud rescue, resulting in an "I got this" bar bill. There were also going to be the additional costs of adding functioning seat belts, a new winch cable for potential crevasse rescues, and a roof rack to store the portable generator and survival gear necessary for mankind's impending doom. I wanted the house. He wanted the truck.

"Fine. You buy your 110 Defender, and I will buy the perfect house for our family—but before we close the deal, I want terms. This truck is your birthday, Christmas, and Father's Day presents for the next ten years."

"Done."

He sprinted away to his computer to plot a spreadsheet that would compare and contrast every available Land Rover for purchase until he found, The One.

He has *his* truck and it sits proudly in the driveway of *my* house. It's black with stamped metal, a winch, right-hand drive, four-wheel drive, decals, trim, and a snorkel. Yes, a snorkel. You need a snorkel if you are going to be traveling in water higher than the engine cap.

Mud Coffee

"Heather, what are you doing?"

"I'm working on my book."

"Come with me, I want to take you out for coffee."

"Really? Why?"

I'd become married-cynical. This meant that yes, my husband would like to take me out for coffee, but it was the middle of the day and we always have coffee brewing at home. I knew this was a setup; I just couldn't figure out what I was being set up for.

"What's going on? Did Twitter break down?"

"No, hurry up, I want to take you out for a coffee."

"Okay, I'm coming." I walked out to the driveway, where he was waiting for me.

"Oh, we're going to take your truck?" I sighed quietly.

"Yeah, get in, it will be fun!"

My husband has a great smile. It's a Cheshire cat grin that goes from ear to ear and lights up his face. He was smiling as he held the door open for me. His energy was infectious, so I climbed into his truck, used the lever to roll down the window, and buckled up.

"Um. You should roll the window up."

"Why?"

"You'll see, it will be fun." I was sure I'd already heard this line.

"I thought we were going to get coffee. Why do I need my window up? Where are you taking me?"

"A shortcut to the coffee place."

I was not this girl. I may do adventure races, paddle in the ocean, go white-water kayaking down a river, climb a mountain, and race across the northern peninsula of Newfoundland, but I don't like adventures with motors. I don't like off-roading, motor boating, dirt biking, or jet-skiing They all have engines that make you go faster than you should in conditions you shouldn't.

The coffee shortcut was a quick foray on an unfinished road through a construction site in the spring. The cut through was narrow with bushy fields on either side and on the main path the spring rains had conveniently created a mini-lake.

"Don't worry honey, that's why we have the snorkel!" he yelled over the whine of the engine.

My face was contorted in a silent scream. As he pulled the steering wheel, we bounced to the roof, and his enthusiasm grew. We careened and slid and bubbled our way to the quaint coffee shop named Ashanti. My husband was happy. He was enjoying a slice of his own happiness, and he was sharing it with me. It was a crisp spring day, and we were both smiling. We got our coffees to go, and my husband promised to take the paved road home. As I sipped my breakfast blend and savored a rare midday outing that involved hanging on to a handle inside the truck, I had to admit I felt good. I felt like I was carefree and young. We were sharing a spontaneous adventure that brought my heart closer to the man I married.

I glanced at my husband. He was grinning and put his hand on my thigh. We were almost at our new house, just sitting at a light waiting for it to turn green. I glanced out the side window as I finished my coffee on this sunny afternoon, and two men in small pick up, were looking at me. They were both in their early thirties wearing jeans and plaid shirts. They were nice looking and they were staring right at me and sort of nodding their heads. I tucked a strand of hair behind my ear and silently wondered if my lipstick was still on. I felt a flush of excitement as I thought about how nice it felt to be admired. It had been a while since boys in cars looked into my window with a wink and a smile.

I looked over again and noticed that these guys were taking it a bit too far. They'd gone from casual smiles to the look of lust and fantasy, and one guy grabbed the crotch of his jeans. I scowled. Who were these pigs? That's when it dawned on me. They weren't looking at me. They could barely see me. Their mouths were open, and one of them was pointing. These guys were salivating over my husband's truck, freshly splattered with mud, the snorkel spewing its exhaust song and the jump seats easily visible from their vantage point. They glanced at me for less than a heartbeat. I could imagine their mocking thoughts and see the look of disappointment on their faces. "She's not cool enough for that truck. Look at her fancy coffee cup—she's probably looking for a cup holder. That truck is awesome. She's probably his mother."

Compromise: his truck and my house. This compromise was about material possessions but compromise is about remembering that your partner is a person with their own dreams and desires. What really made us happy that morning on our ride to the coffee shop was sharing some time together on a fantastic day. It reminded me that the relationship slice is bound by love, like and compromise.

Love, sex, communication, common bonds, differences, fights, power struggles, right, wrong, vacations, roles, rules, and compromise are all ingredients of the relationship slice. Houses, cars, appearances, and appliances are all blended carefully to make the relationship slice work without destroying who we are as individuals. It's like a fabulous lemon meringue pie—simultaneously sour and sweet with layers of complexity. It's a slice of pie that gives me enormous pleasure. Love, respect, and compassion are a large part of the ingredients list, but compromise and managing expectations are the key to not murdering your spouse in this relationship recipe. I love my relationship slice. To me, even though I have the same flavor every day, it's ever-changing by the amount of lemon and sugar, bitter and sweet added over the years.

My husband's LandRover 110 Defender, circa 1985.

CHAPTER NINE

* * *

Family: One and Done—Two and Through—Three and Crazy

The family slice is, bar none, the most complex slice in the giant pie of life. It's a recipe that has no set ingredients, no preparation manual, and no cooking instructions—get married and have babies, don't get married but have babies, accidentally have a baby, or plead with the fertility gods to give you a baby.

I have three daughters. Each one fills a different place in my heart. Their personalities are as complex and diverse as their fingerprints are unique. Their gift to me has been the living mirror they create as they reflect my own best and worst traits. I'm hopeful that I can send my girls off into the world armed with good information, enough self-love, and generous amounts of respect and compassion for both themselves and others. But I'm scared that those qualities won't be enough. That no matter what I do, no matter how hard I try, they will still face disappointment, suffer from broken hearts, face dangers I couldn't predict, and enter adulthood in a world that I haven't been able to baby-proof.

Oh Baby

The morning I gave birth to my first daughter, I awoke with an incurable desire to drink orange juice, about a half gallon of it. I couldn't stop; it was like a sugary river of euphoria flowing down my throat and cooling the inside of my belly. Every time I took a drink, I wanted more. I was on my fourth glass when the phone rang.

"Hey you, how's it going?" Tina asked.

"I'm just sitting here, a giant human, swollen like the Hindenburg. Ten days till due date, yeah, I'm goin'...Agh! Oh, seriously? Agh. Arrghhh!"

"What's wrong? Are you having the baby?"

"Wow, my water broke and I had a serious contraction."

"Oh my God! Oh my God, you're going to have your baby today!"

Tina and I have been best friends for over twenty years. On this day, she was living two thousand miles away. I was the first to get pregnant, and now I would be the first to chart the path of labor and delivery, all without her by my side.

"Ohhaahg. Oh my God. I have to get off the phone. Oh lord." I clutched the receiver like it was a lifeline.

"What? No, okay, yes. Call someone else! Hurry! Call me back!" That was the last thing Tina said before I slipped to the floor in agony.

My husband was home that day, and when he heard me drop to my knees and cry out, he raced upstairs. "Are you okay?"

"No, I'm dying, and if this is only the start of labor, I need you to kill me right now." Then I vomited every drop of orange juice onto the beige carpet.

"Arghhh—ohhhhhhh"—I started panting—"um ughhhhhhh—whhh-hooooo whhooooo"

"What can I do?"

"I don't know. Get the bag. No, wait, help me. Wait, get the car. Arghhhha—ahhha hmmmm ughhsar—ohhhhhhhh."

"Okay, I'll take the bag to the car. Can you get downstairs?"

"Yes, no, yes—just go!"

I watched him disappear down the stairs out to the front. He was taking forever. When he finally bounded back up the stairs, I'd crawled my way to the bathroom.

"What took you so long?"

"I was putting in the car seat."

"Nine months you had to put the car seat in, and you're doing it now? Ughh barf—ohh, kill meeeeee pleeeease!"

"Come on, let me get you to the car."

"I'm fine. I can make it."

Mark knew I couldn't make it to the car on my own, but he shrugged with the knowledge that whatever he said would be wrong.

"Oh, I have to stop. I can't get down the stairs. There's another one coming. Arghhhhhhhhhhhhhhhh."

As I kneeled down, pressed against the stairs, it occurred to me that we might not make it to the "birthing suite" with the television, the whirlpool, and the lovely medicine cabinet filled with pain-relieving drugs. Where were my twenty-four hours of labor promised to me in birth preparedness class? Where were the warning signs and the cramps and all the other milestones that were supposed to lead up to labor? Instead, all I had was what felt like intestinal torture.

"Please drive faster. Can you drive faster, *pleeeease*?" With each contraction my face contorted into a twisted, horrible mess, my hand gripped the inside handle on the door of the truck, and I panted like a dog trapped in a hot car.

"I want to get us there alive. This is not the time to drive crazy."

"Drive crazy? I'll make you crazy when I have this baby in the car on the worst highway in the world. DO YOU WANT TO SEE CRAZY? Aghhh oghhhhh blahg whooooo haa—haaa."

I couldn't figure out why my husband, a police officer, couldn't call in an escort for his laboring wife. What about all those high-speed chase maneuvers he'd told me about? You'd swear he worked for the A-Team, but right then, it was like he worked for Meals on Wheels.

As we rolled up to the hospital, he asked, "Where do you want me to park?"

"Here. Right here. Let me out before I explode."

Being no stranger to 911 situations, he pulled up to the emergency door and adeptly handled the flood of people that eagerly tried to avert us from parking in the ambulance zone. A kind orderly whisked me into a wheelchair while Mark went to park the car. I arrived at the birthing floor alone.

"What's your name, darling?"

"Heather." Pant, pant. Die, die.

"What's your last name?" Her voice was edgy, like she thought I was an idiot. I wanted to scream, *Of course I'm an idiot. Only idiots have babies! Stupid, stupid, stupid.*

An older nurse saw the look on my face. "Shirley, come here. I think we've got an active one!"

Active one? Active, like "enjoys running 5Ks and bike rides in the park?" Why was she smiling? What was she talking about? They moved me into the smallest room in the hospital. It was smaller than my closet, but it was supposed to be for a quick examination so they could send me off to the right place—the place with soft lights and tranquilizers. "Okay, honey, get up on this bed."

Breathe, breathe. Die, die.

"I can't. Can't someone help me? Can I go to the bathroom?"

My last sentence sent them scurrying. Suddenly there were two extra people in the room.

"No, you can't go to the bathroom."

"Why? Please, I have to go."

The pleading in my voice was like a three-year-old child's plaintive request. They'd heard it before and were immune to my query.

"We're just going to see how far along you are. Try to relax."

I think they liked me because I showed up with the bun in my oven almost baked, and without any work to do, I was ready to serve up a baby. These days, very few hospital births are unmedicated or "natural" births. I was an anomaly, not by choice but by chance.

"Okay, great! You're nine centimeters."

"But I just got here!"

"I know, isn't that great? Just one more centimeter and you can start pushing."

"No. Please. Epidural."

I'd been reduced to one word at a time. The contractions were on top of each other, and I needed to leave so that someone else could have this baby.

"Sorry, you're too far along. No time for an epidural now."

It was like she was giddy. I could hear the voice in her head cheering as she buzzed about the room: *Yeah! An active one that's ready for game time! Let's go, team!*

"Not. Fair. Hate. This."

I lapsed into silence between contractions. Otherwise, I was an ungodly mess—grunting, panting, sweating, or screaming.

"Try not to make so much noise. You need to push down with your breath, and if you are letting out sound, you aren't pushing hard enough."

Oh lord, if I could talk right now, I would chop you to pieces with breath knives. Not pushing hard enough! I was a Canada Games gold medalist! I could clean and jerk the ultrasound machine, and you don't think I'm pushing hard enough?

But I couldn't talk. I couldn't say anything. Where was Tina? She would tell them about every one of my sporting accolades and that they shouldn't tell me I needed to work harder. I was pretty sure my life essence was fading, and I was okay with that. I acutely understood why women died in childbirth—because it was easier.

After a few million pushes and the thought of torturing the woman who said I wasn't trying hard enough, out came my baby. We didn't know if we were having a boy or a girl, because we wanted it to be a surprise. By the time she was born, I didn't care if we had a sea otter; I was happy to be alive. The entire experience spanned a total of ninety minutes from orange-juiced carpet to an eight-pound, six-ounce pumpkin we called Clara, born on October 31.

Tribes

The task of bringing life into the world is an extraordinary experience no matter how you achieve it—C-section, natural childbirth, at home, under water, with a doula, in a taxi—it doesn't matter, because you did it. Although labor and delivery is the pinnacle of pregnancy, there is a certain amount of shock that comes with the realization that you are now the lifetime owner of a baby. There is no book or seminar that can prepare you for the journey that comes after delivery. Forget *What to Expect When You're Expecting*—there needs be a book titled *What to Expect When You Have Absolutely Zero Idea What You Are Doing*. Birthing a baby is merely the first step on the child-rearing staircase, a staircase that spirals up to the sky and beyond. After Clara was born, I realized that reading about what to do with a baby offered very little assistance in real life. I didn't need any more pamphlets telling me what to do; I needed a steering committee, a cleaning crew, a grocery shopper, and dedicated night staff to help me. I needed a tribe.

Like most women after giving birth, I was left alone in my hospital room with just my baby and my instincts. My instincts had never been so devoid of answers as the nurse handed me my swaddled baby burrito. My instincts felt joy and delight, but they didn't know anything about nipple cream, breast pads, fat pants, and breast pumps. My instincts wanted to be surrounded by a maternal group of women with wisdom and advice that could help me in this perplexing climb to motherhood. My instincts wanted to be hugged and brought vast amounts of food and tabloid magazines. I longed for someone to tell me I was doing okay, hand me a glittering tiara, and gently whisper that sleeping was now a thing of the past. Every new mom should be enveloped, cherished, and treated like a goddess, but sometime in the last millennium, we've lost our tribe.

Now, new moms find each other in online support groups, mommy forums, and the explosion of mommy blogs. According to recent estimates, there are over four million women blogging about being a parent.[9] The number of times I've Googled perplexing fevers, face rashes, and unjamming things from kids' ears is astounding. I should create a new search engine called Momgle—the traffic would be staggering. On multiple occasions, finding a mom who was going through exactly what I was feeling was lifesaving. Reading the trials of other moms brought everything into perspective. I understood and felt comforted that I wasn't the only one who couldn't handle one more second of a screaming toddler and ran away by hiding in the bathroom.

Perhaps this is the new tribe. I often ask moms-to-be if they are close with their own mothers, because without even one person in your tribe to help you, parenthood is an overwhelming challenge in the first few years. I wish that more women could connect and be helped by others that have walked a mile in the mothering shoes.

Society has painted a picture that you can do it all if you just try hard enough. Moms know it's not true, and yet we still try. We try to breast-feed, shop organic, lose weight, BPA-free our lives, teach with flash cards, toilet train, clean the house, baby proof everything, and remember we are married, all the while managing a career and the household schedule. It's not possible to do it all. I think we could rebuild some of our tribes by getting together with other moms, being honest with each other, and appreciating that some days, your biggest accomplishment is taking a shower. With the help of a tribe, we could catch our breath while we figure out how to climb the next step on our way up the parenting staircase. This primal bond of giving life made me realize I longed to be more than one woman raising this little soul; I longed to be part of this tribe.

God, Santa, and the Tooth Fairy

"Mom, where are we going?"

We were driving across town to their cousin's church.

"We're going to your cousin's first communion."

"Oh. What's that?"

Clara, my oldest, was six at the time. The first two were raised by the Church of Disney, and based on that expense, we were hoping the third would be an atheist.

"Communion is where you eat a bite of Christ."

My entire religious upbringing consisted of a few visits to Sunday school and mandatory attendance at the service held on Christmas Eve.

"You eat a bite of crusts? I don't like crusts."

"No, not crusts, a bite of Christ. Let me start again."

How could I explain the Bible, religion, and sacraments to a kid who thought the baby Jesus should live in a castle with Cinderella?

"In our country, we are lucky enough to believe what we want. Some people believe in God, other people believe we die and come back to Earth as someone else, some people..."

"Well, I believe in God and Santa and the tooth fairy. When our dog Rio died, she went to heaven. We have a picture of the tooth fairy that Daddy took—oh, and how do all those presents get under the tree? And why is there money under my pillow when I lose a tooth? I believe, all right."

I tried again.

"Some people believe that to be closer to God, you go to church so you can talk to Him. Then when you get older, you have these ceremonies that are like stepping-stones. Each step is a bit higher, and it takes you a step closer to

God. That's what Sarah is doing. She is receiving her first communion, like walking up a step closer to God."

"Oh. Is it her birthday?"

"No." I realized as I pulled the car into the parking lot that this discussion was going to need a longer car drive and I was going to need a tutorial on Jesus.

My religious knowledge comes from calling my friend Tina and asking her what the appropriate gift for various religious ceremonies would be. Tina is Catholic and has a firm hold on her faith. She prays, talks to God, and was raised with a level of dogma and guilt that many forward-thinking Catholics of this century feel conflicted about. After she and I had a spirited debate about the possible "better education" offered by Catholic schools, she suggested, "Heather, get your kids started in Sunday school, and then at least they have the option to go to a Catholic school." She continued prodding with a brief monologue on the advantages of Jesus. "Honey, why don't you give the girls a bit of Jesus? It's nice for kids. Sunday school is like a warm hug. They teach them stories from the Bible, and Jesus becomes their friend."

I was hesitant, because I couldn't even tell you one whole story from the Bible. I knew it rained for forty days and forty nights with two of each animal on Noah's ark—the ark was always a kid pleaser. I knew there was a burning bush, and I was aware that Moses parted the Red Sea, but the 'whys' were a mystery to me. I was certain that if I knew more about religion, I would better understand the conflicts in the Middle East, but I didn't. I depended entirely on my friend for real-world religious answers, and when I needed more God lessons, I consulted Wikipedia.

"T, why is Sunday school nice but the lessons from Catholicism are so—I don't know—angry and scary?"

"Oh, the guilt comes later, but Sunday school is gentle. Jesus is your friend, but then as you learn more, you are told that Jesus gave up his life for you and now you owe him. It's a classic bait and switch."

"Hmm. I might have to stick with public school."

I define myself as an unreligious spiritualist. I want to believe in something, I'm just not sure what. There have been times in my life when I swear that "God" is touching me, and for a fraction of a second it feels like I'm standing outside of myself, looking in. I see and feel perfection; holding each one of my babies for the first time, the quiet of the early morning sunrise, or a mountain hike with my husband are times that living feels like a spark from heaven. The vibrancy I feel bursting out of me is what I think heaven would feel like. So when I have to explain communion; going to church, eating a bite of Christ and celebrating with presents and a party, I have trouble linking my personal feelings with those types of ceremonies. I hope I can find the right words when my kids want to know what I believe.

Now more than ever, kids have answers at their fingertips. If they don't know what something means, they just look it up online. Their BS meters are on high alert, and they sense when you don't know what to tell them. I struggle with this often. Giving my kids answers about the meaning or origin of life is difficult when you don't have your own beliefs in order. Finding answers that are simple enough to understand, yet unravel some of life's more complex issues, is tough. When I scroll through the religious options, there isn't one faith that I want to teach my kids. As a result, I sound confused and wishy-washy when I answer their questions about why there weren't dinosaurs on the ark. If developing a new religion wasn't sure to brand me a nutbar, I would blend the best pieces of each one together and leave sin, Satan, and purgatory to the zealots and the Kool-Aid cults.

In my mind, I see the various deities sitting at a giant round table with microphones like they have at the UN. I would take my place at the lectern and politely ask each deity to lend me a bit of dogma for my collage Bible.

"Hi, God? I'd like to use heaven as one of my religious options. And Buddha, if you don't mind, I'll also take reincarnation, in case I have a penchant for returning to our beloved earth. Oh, and sushi. Who created sushi? Let me tell you, anyone who can sell a rice ball wrapped in seaweed and raw fish must be touched by the hand of God. Yup, I'll keep sushi on the checklist. I'd also like to pick four of the Ten Commandments to add to my à la carte scripture—no killing, lying, stealing, or adultery. Right. Hinduism. I really like karma and the whole 'birth, life, death, rebirth' thing you have. It reminds me of *The Lion King*. Okay, I think that rounds out my beliefs nicely and gives me a starting point with my kids. I might even market it as an e-book for Kindle and hand out pamphlets with the Halloween candy. I'll call it *A Slice o' Faith.*"

I'm thankful that my parents didn't force a religion on me; their approach has given me the chance and the choice to decide what works for me. While religion is about the most polarizing topic I could write about, I want my kids to know that there are a wide range of religious (and non-religious) beliefs throughout the world. By giving my kids information and education I would be giving them the option to choose. I figure they can come to their own conclusions and find a faith (or non-faith) that will meet their needs.

God Camp

It was with good intention and a fair helping of ignorance that my husband and I sent the kids to summer camp at a local church near our house. We really sent them there because it was inexpensive; it was being subsidized by God. I guess more realistically, it was subsidized by those who donated to God's house, but it made no difference to me. By offering a day camp at such a low price, the church gave people like myself, with a stretched budget and a new baby at home, an opportunity for a week of summer without the kids. The camp boasted "daily activities with an eco-friendly theme." Perfect.

I guess it went without saying that an eco-friendly camp held in a church would also include God-friendly activities and lessons about all the stuff God does. At the end of the first day, I picked up the girls and the floodgates opened. Out poured religious questions like the River Ganges with its sin-cleansing current.

"Mommy, God is a man with wings and magic, right?"

"Well, some people think he's a man. Wait, magic? Did they tell you he uses magic?"

"Mommy, when God made all the animals, did he make them in one place and then they all walked to where they live now?"

"Yes. Maybe."

"God made *everything*, right, Mommy? He made us and animals and trees and bugs. Did he make garbage? Why would God make garbage, Mommy?"

"We make garbage. God made other stuff."

"So God made everything but garbage?"

"Yes. No. I don't know."

I'd always envisioned teaching my kids important morals and values and giving them the chance to decide whether they wanted religion in their lives or not. One eight-hour session at church day camp, and they had met God. God was a nice, tidy answer for everything unexplainable. How simple—if my children had God as an answer, I could explain bad things like death and wickedness and tragedy. I could use God to explain things I didn't understand, like rechargeable batteries and Wi-Fi. I could just let them *believe.* They were like little lemming sponges, ready for Christian absorption.

It would be so easy to just go with it. But I couldn't do it. I couldn't do it because I don't have faith in religion. This is not the same as believing in nothing; it's believing in *something* with the absence of a structured guide. The Bible, the Koran, the Torah are all road maps to the various religions. I needed an un-Bible to explain how I felt about a higher spirit.

This is when I decided it was now or never. I would let my kids figure out whether they wanted religion in their lives, but I would give them *my* holy trinity right now, right here in the car.

"Girls, I want to talk to you for a minute. Do either of you know what the most important thing in the world is?"

"Santa?"

"No. The most important thing in the world is love."

"I love you, Mom. Can we have ice cream?"

"No. More than anything, you need to always remember to be loving. Do you know who you should love first?"

"You?"

"No. You need to love *you* first. Love yourself. Then you will have enough love to give to everyone else. Like your family and your friends."

"I love my stuffies and my Littlest Pet Shops."

I forged ahead. "You know when we are all playing together as a family in the living room and we are tickling and laughing and having a great time?"

"Yes."

"That's what love feels like. It's like you wish that time would never stop and the smiles and playtime would go on forever, because it feels so good in your heart. This feeling is the most important thing."

"I get it, Mommy. We love our family and our friends because they are more important than loving toys and stuff, right?"

"Yes, Ellie. Love yourself first, then love others."

"Mom? Can we go buy some toys?"

"No."

The full trinity would have to wait. While we were always trying to impart loving ways on our children, talking about love and being loving was a good start to giving them a mental guide on being good people.

My holy trinity includes love, respect, and compassion. I'm constantly driving home these three ideals to my girls. Although we didn't get to the other two parts in the car that day, we do work on them when there is a fitting moment. Repeatedly, I explain to the girls that each part of the trinity (love, respect, and compassion) is important to see in others, but it is most important to see in their own images first. Respect yourself first, and then show respect for your family, friends, community, and "stuff." Be gentle with yourself and find the compassion to forgive yourself. Once you do this, you will find a greater compassion for others. We work on these ideals when the time arises. We find respect for listening to others and respect for our toys. We look for ways to show compassion for our own mistakes and problems as well as other people's mistakes and misfortunes. Ultimately we try to remember to be loving, and this is a core value in any religion. Sometimes the best lesson is when they remind Mommy to practice the trinity she keeps preaching about.

"BE QUIET, YOU ARE MAKING ME CRAZY." My yelling outbursts happen regularly in the car, in the store, in the kitchen—I guess anyplace that isn't the vacuum of outer space.

"Mom, why are you yelling at us? Remember, the most important thing is love. Yelling is not showing respect or *crompaston.*"

"Compassion, Ellie. Thank you, but you missed the fourth."

"There's no fourth."

"Love, respect, compassion, and silence."

"Mommy, you're funny."

"Shhh."

Joining the Club

A friend of mine called to chat. I think she wanted me to tell her not to have children. She said, "Can I ask you something?"

"Of course."

"Every one of my friends who has children is miserable. Why do people have kids? Your kids are great and everything, but what if I don't like it?"

I was eating while I listened to her. Anyone with children understands that all uninterrupted phone time is considered "free time" by the other parent. If you are using your "free time" chatting, then you should consider multitasking with a snack to ensure that you maximize your allotment.

"Yeah, it does seem like all we do is complain. It's not that we don't love our children, we just don't like them sometimes and it makes us appear miserable." I added the "sometimes" because my friend was part of the uninitiated. She was getting married in two months, and they were planning on starting a family as soon as the last guest found a taxi.

"Right! Exactly. Why have kids when all my girlfriends say they are tired, don't have a career anymore, have gained weight, and hate their husbands?"

I put down my McFat breakfast sandwich and dabbed the crumbs from the counter with my index finger. I paused a moment to think, because my answer was key to her moving forward down the path of parenthood or abandoning the idea altogether.

"Listen hon, you have kids because once you have them, you come to understand that life before kids was never quite as vivid. It would be like trying to tell someone what the color red looks like if they have never seen color. You test every boundary, every idea, and every thought of who you are, and even though everything changes, you would never know this new part of yourself without having had little wrinkled-up bundles of love."

"But what if I'm miserable?" This was where it got tricky. Telling someone on the path to having children that they *won't* be miserable would not be altogether true.

"Of course you'll be miserable."

My answer was met with silence. She was listening and waiting for my explanation. Now I needed a home run. "But you will be part of the Club, and it's a fun club."

"You're scaring me. Part of the Club? How is being miserable and part of a club, fun?"

I wished I could explain it, but I couldn't. You can't explain "the Club" until you are in the club. How do you tell someone what it's like to make a child with the person you love, carry that baby for nine months, give birth, and come to understand what a miracle it is to create life? Then I'd have to describe the incredible moments, triumphs, sadness, worry, and love euphoria that you feel for that child; the stunning, intense, unadulterated joy you have from being together with your baby.

"Listen, of course the Club isn't for everyone. That's something you have to decide. But if the Club was *sooooo* miserable, would I have joined it three times? You can always be a one-time joiner. Most people can't screw that up too badly. You get all the benefits of membership with about a million fewer headaches."

The problem with joining the Club is that there are no trial memberships. You can't get a three-month guest pass to see if you like it before you join for real. I also didn't go on to explain that a one-time membership is not quite the same as a multiple membership. Moms that are, by choice, one-and-done are fully loved and respected for all the new mother struggles, tears, and dreams of a clean blouse, but the rest of us just don't want to know how fast they got back into their skinny jeans.

It's hard to know why so many women desire to have more children when having even one can seem like a weird jail sentence at times. One and done, two and through, three and crazy. What comes after three? Four and my husband is out the door? Five and I'm barely alive? We have three kids. That used to be the average number of children, but stats are showing that most couples aren't even fulfilling the quota of replacing themselves. We are a declining population, which is good if you don't like people, but bad if you like the economy.

This brings me back to the question: if having one baby is tough enough, why on Earth have more? This is a hard question to answer, and an extremely personal one. For us, getting pregnant was as easy as sneezing in a feather factory. We didn't have to think or plan or struggle. No calendars or temperatures or tests or trials. We were lucky. So lucky that our first baby was a surprise, our second baby resulted from a mistimed romantic getaway, and only by the third baby did we make a conscious decision to try again. Maybe we had three kids so we could say at least one of them was planned.

The point is that kids are not for everyone, and that's okay by me. Kids are a game changer, a marriage destabilizer; they can be the undoing of a perfectly happy relationship, turning it into a messy, tired, perpetual fog. I am grateful that, for me, joining this club was easy, but staying in the club requires commitment, patience, self-growth, and a giant well of love.

What Happened to Me?

"I'm not going to change anything when the baby is born. We're planning on getting some help so I can get out and do my exercise, and I'm going to get back to work fairly quickly. You know, it will be good."

I've said those words, and I've heard them from first-time parents repeatedly. Women dream about having a baby for what it will bring to their lives, not what it will take away. You believe that your lifestyle won't change that much just because you're having a baby. Then you actually have a baby.

When I became a mom, something happened to my purpose. It got all mashed up with everyone else's purposes, leaving me with little of my own. I don't think there is a mother around who doesn't wistfully revisit her days before kids with thoughts of "What could I have done? Where would I be now? Would I be at the peak of my career? Would I be traveling and learning about other countries and cultures? Would I be a kinder, skinnier, happier person if I didn't have kids?" I can't answer these questions, because I can't change the past. However, I can tell you how I managed.

Some women are destined to be moms as a vocation. When asked what they wanted to be when they grew up, they said, "I want to be a mommy." Sometimes I wish I were one of them. When I was younger I wasn't so sure I wanted kids, but sometime in my late twenties I felt the desire to become a parent.

Now, as a mother of three, I still struggle with the responsibility of guiding small humans through the complex mores of our times. Finding love for my children is easy—I just open my heart and calm all the noise around me. I know the love is always there because that's what being a mother feels like to me, but until I shake being on the mommy-treadmill of doing a thousand things everyday it's hard for my kids to hear or feel that love. I've come to understand that it's the noise that creates the dissonance within my role as a mother. The pervasive parental advice and conflicting directives are what make it hard for any mom or parent to silence the inner critic and just enjoy spending some time with our kids. The volume of information available about schooling, home-schooling or un-schooling, nutritional advice, allergy advice, and the extracurricular merry-go-round that we put ourselves and our kids on is overwhelming. Cutting through the info-noise and finding my own voice of reason has awakened the joy and love in raising my children. Until I could reconcile what seemed to be the norm; a complicated balancing act of kids, work and countless schedules - with what I wanted - uncomplicated family time and a sense of raising children that were working towards independence, I wasn't going to find much happiness in this slice. I rediscovered the answer that silenced both the external and internal critics: common sense. And nowhere has this innate gift of mankind become more lost than in our schools.

School is one of those weird areas where you know your kids are learning, but you aren't sure if they are learning what will help them be a productive person. This trickles into my subconscious and pokes at my common sense organ. I don't care that much about my kids' homework, because I'm not entirely sure that doing homework is that beneficial. My common sense says that they have enough time in school to learn the basics but my flagging parental self-esteem wonders if I'm doing enough and maybe it's worth the after school struggle to force the kids into algebra submission. But it kills me. The process of getting them to do extra work instead of spending non-yelling time together doesn't feel worth the struggle. I have a strong ability in math and I can tell you I've never used anything more than the basics for much in my life. I can't figure out if I'm lazy or giving my kids an advantage when I miss various events that happen every day at their school. While I've done my share of getting the kids ready for countless school fun days, I've also forgotten or not known about a multitude of crazy hair days, inside-out days, twin days, popcorn days, pink shirt days, and assemblies on courage, honesty, and compassion days. Somewhere along the line, I stopped caring because it felt like one more thing I needed to organize for my kids that didn't make sense. My common sense said these things are ridiculous, but the other voice in my head said, "Other parents seem to find the time to help their kids, what's wrong with you?" The true crime is that if I had taken the time to teach them how to be more personally responsible, these fun-days would have been a choice for them to participate because they had also chosen to prepare for them. So I continue to flex my common sense where it seems some is lacking and other days I cave into what is easier and just trudge to the dollar store for non permanent, hair coloring spray.

These events make me wonder how much of my own self-worth is being traded to keep up with what doesn't feel like a valuable trade-off. I've become resentful of taking up extra time to prepare stuff for these endless theme days, when what I really wish is that someone cared what *I* wanted. This is part of my internal battle between being Mommy and being Heather. I truly want what's best for my babies, but not always at the price of my own well-being.

"Hey, Mom?"

"Yes, babe?"

"What would make you happy?"

It was bedtime, and I was finalizing the pre-bedtime freedom checklist: pack lunches, yell at kids, clean the kitchen, yell at kids, tidy front door, yell at kids.

"What would make me happy? Oh, I don't know. It would make Mommy happy if you would go to sleep."

"But I'm not tired."

"Then it would make Mommy happy if you would pack your own lunch."

"But I don't know how."

"Okay. What if I just asked you to eat your lunch when you're at school? Could you at least eat your lunch?"

"I could try, but I don't always have time. We're too busy playing or talking."

"I see. Well, could you tell your teacher that Mommy isn't going to send lunch to school anymore, because you don't eat any of it, and not to call Child Services, because I'm not intentionally starving you, and I would just rather never make another school lunch that you didn't eat for the rest of my life, okay?"

"Okay. Mommy? Who do you want me to tell them to call?"

That's why they don't ask what would make me happy, because the answer is so complicated. I love the family slice. I also loved my life before kids, and I am searching for a way to love this 'new me' after kids. Dedicating time and energy to the family slice brings incredible value and personal reward, but it is the slice that takes the most out of me and demands my time and attention like no other piece of the pie.

As I question daily what happened to the person I was before kids, another realization clarifies in my mind.

It goes so fast.

I am constantly struggling between the roles of being a nurturing mom and an individual soul who allows myself time and energy to take care of my personal goals. The realization that my kids are growing up so quickly makes me pause to wonder if I should stop trying so hard to be both and enjoy this stage with my kids more. "It goes so fast" is the most repeated parenting cliché since Grok painted pictures on the cave wall—pictures of children leaving the cave, taking baskets filled with animal skins and Ikea bone furniture, while their parents watch and cry.

Having children inexplicably warps your sense of time. Toddlers make the days pass like a slow-motion torture wheel of to-dos. The hours between 5 p.m. and bedtime move like old people in the park doing tai chi. Yet every year that passes seems to disappear like cookies in the cupboard. You blink and they're gone. My current status as a mommy with toddlers, a stage that requires hyper-involved parenting, is quickly moving toward being told by my kids to get out of their room and that I'm stupid.

During the early years, I wondered if I would survive. In all the chaos and mess, it was easy to lose the 'me' that started this journey. I wanted to reconnect with the intelligent, powerful, funny person inside of this mommy, and I resolutely refused to be swallowed up by everyone else's needs. When I say to my kids, "Mommy is a person too," I hope to show my girls that women are more than maids and nose wipers and short-order cooks. I hope to show them that being a woman is about more than taking care of the thousand little details of life; it's also about embracing the fun and joy that raising a family brings. Being a woman with a family still means you are an individual person with goals and dreams separate from your role as a mother. What I've come to learn is that if you lose yourself—the part of you that makes you happy—in the process of raising your kids, you will be dissatisfied with both your roles. If you try to cram yourself into a mold, a societal idea of what having children and being a woman means, you will fail on both counts. You need to find your own balance point—the fulcrum between the old you and the new you. Each of us has our own tolerance for mommyhood, but you will serve no one if you try to pretend you can be everything to everyone.

To me, these years are precious and fleeting, and while I'm on the tapering side of the incredible demands of raising babies and toddlers, I can only imagine that soon I will be looking back, yearning for times that were simpler. I will wonder what happened to years between holding my babies wearing feet-attached sleepers and sending them off into the world where pjs are silky short-shorts with spaghetti strap tops.

Finding a bit of happiness within the family slice is not difficult for me. If I squint my eyes and look past the crumbs and sticky fingers and broken pie dish, I can see the happiness everywhere. It's in their laughter and their tears, their triumphs and their struggles. Having children opened a secret door in my heart that was never available to me before. It's a door to crazy, unconditional love; an insane, intense, almost stupid feeling you have inside that makes you wacko if you think about anyone or anything hurting your child.

Having children is like owning a new set of eyes. These new eyes give you a chance to experience something for the first time—again. You see an ant with your two-year-old and watch it like you did when you were a child, because it *is* fascinating. You're reminded that picking an ice cream flavor is mind-blowing, and eating the ice cream should be done while sitting down and focusing on every lick. Nature, machines, food, playtime—every bit of it is an incredible new experience for kids, and having these new eyes is a reminder to see the world through a different lens. The lens of a child changes your perspective. It reminds you to slow down, enjoy the view, and get excited about life's greatest wonders. As parents, we have to remember to enjoy this slice while our little babies still want hugs and help and a moment to shine in our eyes. Children do change your life, and no matter what you said before having them, you have a newfound view of the world that you couldn't have seen or felt without this messy, frustrating, tiring addition to your journey. I won't ever be the person I was, but I am working on finding a new normal to go with my new set of eyes.

Having children is like being served a giant slice of humble pie. As a parent I've been made to eat every judgment—spoken or thought—that I've ever inflicted on another parent. By experiencing firsthand the temper tantrum of a two-year-old, the exhaustion and fear of a sick baby in the middle of the night, and the protectiveness every mom feels for their child, I've come to understand that the best I can do is lend an ear, give a suggestion if asked, or just be there for support of another parent in need.

Humble pie used to be the pie of servants and the poor. It consisted of the entrails, large organs, and other parts of animals that the upper crust wouldn't eat. I think the modern-day equivalent would be hot dog pie. If having children means eating entrail pie, hot dog pie, or humble pie, then I promise I will dive wholeheartedly into this flaky, crusted slice filled with

Oscar Mayer bits and drizzled with ketchup. I will chew it slowly while I savor the thought that this is one slice of pie that, as difficult and trying as it seems, I would never want to miss tasting.

Clara (6 yrs), Fiona (6 months) and Ellie (4 yrs) – my little angels.

CHAPTER TEN

* * *

Health: Fu*k You, Fat

There are all kinds of being fat, but there is one kind that is the same for everyone: *fatter than you were.*

It doesn't matter whether you have fifteen or fifty pounds to lose—most people would like to return to some ideal weight they used to be. Wanting to change your appearance through weight loss is the same as saying, "I want some of my happy back."

The health slice is metaphorically, a hefty piece of the happiness pie. We've all heard people say, "You're nothing without your health," and although this is true, the word "health" has come to mean many things.

The simplest definition of health is not being sick. Take this further, and you'll find the healthy fitness folk. They work out, eat nutritious food, manage their stress, and declare themselves to be healthy. One step further, and you'll find the health gurus who believe the world is a toxic environment and move to Belize to live off the grid and recycle their recycling. The definition of health has a wide range of meaning.

Thousands of books have been written in an attempt to serve up the perfect health-slice recipe. For every book that tells you eating fat is good, there are three telling you fat will clog your arteries like a hairball in the drain. Drink coffee; don't drink coffee; try a coffee enema. Take vitamin D; don't take vitamin D, but lay in the sun with sunscreen. The lists of contradictory advice are endless. It's clear that our bodies are individual and complex, and medical science is an ongoing pursuit that still grapples with that complexity. Health can be a confusing slice.

In contrast to the global warming debate, there doesn't seem to be any controversy about whether or not people in North America are getting fatter. There are clear indicators that the population is expanding its girth, and most people would agree that carrying extra weight can make you feel both physically and mentally miserable. The question remains: How do we reverse this global fattening?

"Tina, sometimes I look in the mirror and can't believe that the person I'm looking at is me. It's like I'm wearing a fat suit, but I'm not. I'm not even looking in a full-length mirror. I can't imagine seeing my whole body all at once. I want to hide."

"Oh, don't say that. You're beautiful."

I ignored my friend's compliment and pushed on with my pity party. "Sometimes I put deodorant between my thighs so that if I'm wearing a dress, my thighs won't chafe and rub a hole to the bone."

"Oh, sweetie, you just had another baby. Be kind to yourself."

"Thank you, but that was a year and a half ago. I can't keep thinking that it's going to evaporate. I watch the other exercise-y moms, and I see how they get in their training time and their girls' nights out. What am I doing wrong?"

"Maybe you just don't care?"

"What? Of course I care." But when I pause to think about her question, I'm startled by my realization. "Oh, no, what if I don't care anymore? Gosh, you're right. I don't care as much as I used to, at least until I look at myself after a shower. Then I care a whole lot."

"Yes, and then you put on your pants and a shirt and you say 'screw it,' because you have a thousand things to do and your fat will have to wait."

"Yeah, but I wish it came with a zipper."

Being fatter than I used to be feels like I'm wearing a sign that says, "Please judge me and all my life choices." It makes me feel sad, angry, demoralized, and—well, fat.

Even as a lifelong health and fitness proponent, I'm exhausted by our nation's obsession with thinness and my own struggle to return to my happy weight. The mainstream media continues to pump out misinformation, telling us that the answer is to eat less and exercise more. This has become a difficult solution to swallow, since there is clearly evidence that tells us there is more to the problem than just an unbalanced equation. Hormones, age, stress, fat receptors, insulin resistance, leptin, and cortisol are all making the fat loss headlines. Each one appears to be a piece of the puzzle that will uncover the solution to this giant fat experiment in which millions of people have unwittingly become participants.

It's equally disturbing that being overweight is identified with being lazy and unmotivated. The predominant belief is that if you just *tried harder*, you would see results. I've worked with dedicated, motivated clients who are exercising more and eating less, and they still have a terrible time losing weight. Whether you have 20 or 120 pounds to lose, the weight loss struggle becomes a constant battle.

If you were hoping that I would give you a simple, one-sentence solution to your weight loss dilemma, I can't. It doesn't exist. For some people, the traditional prescription of eating less and exercising more *does* work. For others, it's about setting attainable goals and staying focused. A huge number of people who follow low-carb diets, such as the Atkins diet or the paleolithic diet, do see results, but keeping the weight off is another battle altogether. For some people it's simple; for others it's not. If a monthly injection that infused people's bodies with skinny DNA was available, I'm sure there would be a lineup for it that would stretch to the moon.

The rotund elephant in the room is that 60 percent of the nation is obese or overweight.[10] Are all of these people lazy, slovenly individuals? Sixty percent of 335 million is 200 million people who, according to conventional wisdom, have no self-control and do nothing but stuff their faces while they lay about wondering which pair of stretch pants to put on. It seems a bit unrealistic to assume that being fat comes solely from a person's lack of desire to change. Fixing an obese nation will require more than each individual's desire to be healthier; it will require a logical, dedicated cultural shift in the way we view health. I didn't come to this conclusion after reading a few articles or trendy weight loss books. It turns out that I needed to be hit on the head with the fat stick.

I Learned That It Wasn't So Simple

This is the hardest chapter for me to write, because I am fatter than I used to be. I used to be an athletic machine—I wasn't just fit, I was *über*fit. This made me immune to the creeping obesity that often starts when you are in your mid twenties and continues until you're old enough to nod off in a chair in front of the television. Counting calories, doing aerobics, and watching an upwardly shifting scale were other people's problems. I believed what I was taught: eat less, exercise more, and you will be thin and healthy. What's not to believe?

A lot, as it turns out.

After university I returned home and started working as a personal trainer. It was meant to be a stopgap between graduation and a career. The lack of available jobs and the nation's insatiable desire to be thin turned this gig into my profession. I was fired up and ready to help my clients vanquish their ugly fat. As a national-level athlete and a science graduate, I could solve their problem of being overweight because I was qualified and I was healthy. I was more than healthy—I was healthy and an asshole.

As a personal fitness guru, I would start by assessing my client's objectives. "Tell me, Susan, what is your end goal?"

Susan, a woman in her mid thirties, would grab the roll of fat skimming above the waistband of her tights and say, "I want to get rid of *this*." She would squeeze and squish her fat like she hoped it would flatten or rub off.

I'd feel embarrassed. I couldn't believe she would squeeze her fat so openly. I would then ask, "Okay, I see. How much weight would you like to lose?"

"Oh, about thirty pounds. You know, I used to be thin. I used to look like you."

My first asshole thought was, *What happened? How did you gain thirty pounds? I can't picture you in your twenties. Really, how does someone just let themselves go?* Of course, I never said this. At twenty, I couldn't understand how people gained so much weight when they used to look like me. *Pah! They probably never looked like me.* See? Asshole.

I expanded my asshole repertoire by telling clients that if they weren't reaching their exercising and eating goals, they "didn't want it enough." I explained that if they were truly dedicated to the program and did what I said, they would achieve results. I furthered this line of thinking by gently saying, "Sometimes we think we want something, but not bad enough to really do the work needed to get the results." I told most clients that they could fit in sixty minutes of exercise every day. No excuses. I was a fit-bitch asshole.

Early in my career I didn't understand the complexity of grown-up life struggles. Clients would unload tragic tales of marital heartbreak, sick children, or life sadness, and I would listen and nod, but I had no context in which to place their stories. I couldn't empathize in a way that had any meaning, because at twenty-three, I didn't have much filling in any slices of my life pie. The only thing I was good at was my health slice, and if you were looking for your own *Biggest Loser* tough-girl trainer, I was it.

Over the years, clients repeatedly told me that their goal was to be healthier. While this sounded logical, I found that unless clients were literally dying, their goal was not to achieve health gains—their real goal was to be thin.

Here's a translation of clients' code words. A client would say, "I want to be healthy."

Bullshit. "Healthy" meant "thin."

"I want to be more energetic."

"Energetic" meant "thin."

"I want to feel better."

"Feel better" meant "feel thin in my pants."

No one booked an appointment with me, laid their heart on the line, and paid me money to make them healthy. They wanted me to make them skinny. They wanted to return to a weight that in another time equaled happiness for them. Even my skinny clients just wanted to be skinnier. You can shake your head and disagree, but no matter how much their blood pressure went down, their cardio capacity went up, and their muscular strength increased, they would still grip their stomachs and ask me, "When am I going to lose *this*?"

I came to be an expert in my field after I had developed my own "this."

My struggle started with my first two pregnancies, which were very close together. Our first baby had some health issues that kept her from sleeping more than twenty minutes at a time. Screw Dr. Sears; to hell with the *No Cry Sleep Solution*; "suck it" to all the good advice bestowed upon me by other mothers with babies who slept. My firstborn might as well have been Gordon Gekko—her intensity and inability to sleep almost killed me. This was the start of what I saw as my demise.

Recently there has been a significant increase in the number of studies showing that without adequate sleep, weight loss can be close to impossible.[11] Sleep affects cortisol levels in your body. When you are sleep-deprived, cortisol levels increase. Increased cortisol levels lead to increased insulin levels in the bloodstream. Increased insulin levels leads to increased fat storage. With the level of sleep deprivation I reached, I could have starred in my own *Fat Storage Wars* TV show. *Can I hear seventy-five dollars for this chunky unit?*

Baby Clara gave me the first ten pounds never to leave. A second baby eighteen months later added ten more pounds that seemed happy to stay. I was an entrepreneur running my own business with no maternity benefits, and so my new life as a mother combined with a constant work load and a serious lack of sleep came together to create the perfect fat storm. After sneaking in one more pregnancy at the age of thirty-nine, I became the fatty triad: old, tired, mom.

This could not be me. This was never me. But now, quietly, stealthily, this had become me. I hated this me. Start, stop, on the wagon, off the wagon—this was my life. I would start on a healthy eating plan on Monday, and by Thursday I was throwing my hands in the air and crying in the shower. I couldn't do it. I couldn't sacrifice any more. I was too overwhelmed, too busy, and everyone wanted a piece of my time, my energy, and my soul. I was too tired to eat right and exercise; some days I was too tired to sleep.

Only then was I able to understand why it was so hard for middle-aged women with two kids, a spouse, a full-time job, aging parents, and a house to manage to get in shape. Because only then did I become one of them.

What I learned over the course of twenty years was that the confusing information about healthy eating, the "more exercise is better" philosophy, and the lack of research about sleep and hormones are huge contributing factors to being unsuccessful at weight loss. I learned that both eating and exercising habits are heavily influenced by well-funded food marketing campaigns and fitness industry deceptions.[12] We are fighting an evolutionary battle between our DNA and our current lifestyle. Our bodies want to store fat, and our first-world lifestyle gives our bodies every chance to be successful. This is why the weight loss battle feels relentless. Survival of the fittest doesn't mean so much in a world where security comes from a sharp eye for investment rather than a sharp stick for hunting.

The simplest answer is not to gain the weight in the first place.

Duh.

I've almost paid my karmic dues. Skinny-bitch asshole has hung up her hat and is looking for a way out of her Spanx. I was a woman who saw the world through the rose-colored lens of youth and vitality. I preached without having walked through the valley. I extolled thinness without having seen the other side. Just maybe I have paid enough, and the fat gods will let me have my waist back. I will rise again, but this time I will rise with grace, experience, and empathy. I will be prepared with perspective, compassion, and knowledge when I come to you with the question, "What are your goals?"

This time I will have the right program and answers that address your personal situation—solutions that work when your days are long and your nights are short; ideas that work when you have a young family, changing hormones, and work stresses. I will be ready to listen and understand when you tell me, "I used to look like you."

Fixing the Problem

Healthy eating has become a mystery to most people. Who can keep up with the changing recommendations posted by news media on a daily basis? Don't eat wheat. Gluten's bad for your gut. Corn is killing you. Genetically modified foods are the end of the world. Eat meat. Don't eat meat. Eat for your blood type, eat like a South Pacific surfer, eat like a caveman, count things and then eat them, weigh things, block things, calculate things, and then don't eat them. Maybe just eat the box? The box has fiber. Stop! Fiber is not good for you—it promotes leaky gut. Leaky gut? Medium-chain triglycerides, trans fats, hidden fats, good fats, trim the fat, eat the fat, don't heat the fat—oh, it all gives me a big fat headache. No wonder we're miserable; we're afraid to eat, and then, ironically, we eat to solve the problem. Why is everyone in North America so fat? The solution should be simple. It used to be simple, but now it's not.

In North America, food is the problem, and at the same time food is the answer—the answer to *everything*. We eat when we are lonely, sad, and depressed. We eat when we are happy, joyous, and celebratory. Food is the answer to everything, because slowly, food has been promoted from being a wonderful addition to an event, to being the main event.

Can you imagine a Super Bowl party without nachos, chili dogs, wings, beer, or cheesy puff balls? It might as well be called the Super Eat

Fatty Sugary Foods and Watch Funny Commercials Bowl. There are twelve thousand cooking shows, and yet no one cooks. Who has the time to grab fresh herbs and a giant wok, and ensure that the veggies are organic, the oil won't denature at high temps, and the bowls are BPA-free? No wonder so many people take Ativan; it helps relieve the anxiety of figuring out what to eat. We dream about being cooking goddesses and better homemakers. We are shown "five easy, homemade meals" and thirty-minute dinner makeovers that remind us of one more way we fall short in trying to find success with our health—one more way we aren't living up to a perceived standard that is unattainable by the average working family in North America. Yet we still try. Everyone I know wants to feel better about their food choices.

As the stress in my life piled up, food was there for me in its uniquely satisfying way, and it had no rival. Food didn't judge me or look at me with disdain; it didn't tell me to try harder or work smarter or be more. It was just there waiting for me, to give me a happy feeling within an instant of reaching my savory, salty, and sweet taste buds.

This is a conversation I've had more than once with different friends:

"Sarah, are you going to have dessert?"

"Damn right I am. I've been so good for the past two weeks. No sugar and working out! I'm going to reward myself with something decadent."

"Me too!"

Dessert eating loves company—an accomplice to the event of ordering something sinful. "What are you going to get?"

"There are so many good choices. I want something chocolaty and rich, with gooey sauce and some crunch to it, like a cookie or caramel crackle. Something I can dream about later tonight." I understood her sentiments completely.

"Oh, that sounds so good. I'll get a cheesecake and we can each try half."

Being a mom to three young kids, running a business, and living on a budget means sometimes it feels like there are no other rewards. "Sleep" is a word reserved for some other theoretical time in my life. I don't buy new clothes because I'm still fat. I'm still fat because everything seems to be my responsibility. I know I shouldn't use food as a reward, but a sleeve of cookies is cheap and delicious and doesn't talk to me while I fill my face with its sugary goodness. It's inexpensive, instant gratification with an emotional upswing; eating my emotions is just a practical solution. Social eating, emotional eating, and secret cookie eating are only one small part of the health slice dilemma. There's more, and it's big.

The More and The Big

Science is catching up with what our bodies have been telling us for the last forty years. Sugar, fast foods, and fake foods are killing us. My conclusions have come from my observations and experience working as a personal trainer with long-term clients. I draw upon other experts for their articles, studies, and reviews to help me guide my clients. Gary Taubes, author of *Good Calories, Bad Calories,* has cracked the scientific world wide open with his look at why we are fat. Michael Pollen, in *The Omnivore's Dilemma,* has done an incredible service educating people on the real business of eating. Mark Sisson, author of *The Primal Blueprint,* and Robb Wolf, author of *The Paleo Solution,* have changed people's lives with their advice. Of course, any advice or suggestions made in this chapter should not be pursued without the written consent of your doctor—who is probably also fat.

How did the caramel get in the Caramilk bar? I don't know, but I do have the recipe for how the fat got into the obese nation. North America is covertly manufacturing fat people.

Recipe for an Obese Nation

Ingredients:

20 billion dollars

157,000 agricultural subsidies

270 million tons of corn

313 million bushels of wheat

Inactivity (a generous helping)

Entitlement (a dash for flavor)

Fear (enough to spread around)

Equipment:

One industrial-sized marketing oven

Preparation:

1. In a large bowl, put billions of dollars every year into farms that grow corn, soybeans, and wheat. Add these ingredients to a jumbo food industry supported by subsidized agriculture. Blend together to create food-like substances at artificially reduced prices. (See: Ho Hos and margarine.)

2. Bake these food-like substances in an industrial-sized marketing oven. This process requires time and constant attention. Do not let common sense intrude on a half-baked food concept. (Cheese-in-the-crust pizza didn't happen overnight.)

3. Remove from oven. Add a healthy dash of entitlement. (Food is meant to be eaten when dispirited or spirited.)

4. Allow others to sample the results for free. (See: Costco and direct sample mailing.)

5. Share this recipe with your children. Promote these food-like substances in schools, movie theaters, and after-school specials to capture the next generation's potential for grandiose pant sizes.

Note: This recipe is best served with inactivity and a side of fear-based living—fear of terrorism, fear of germs, fear of failing, and fear of Nancy Grace.

It sounds like a conspiracy theory, but it's not. The recipe amounts are real numbers that add up to an excellent formula for creating an obese nation.

My Unsecret Formula

It's not all doom and gloom. There is hope. Just because it's hard to lose weight doesn't make it impossible, and even if it is hard, that doesn't mean you shouldn't work towards better health. I have an unsecret formula I use with my clients and for myself. Ken Follett may have written *The Pillars of the Earth*, but I have written *The Four Pillars of Less Girth.*

EAT—SLEEP—BREATHE—MOVE

Four things. You can spell them all, and they are mostly free.

EAT:

1. Eat real food. "Food" doesn't need a label. You should be able to count the number of steps that it takes to make an ingredient for your dinner. Raw vegetable would be one step. Cooked veggie, two. Cooked vegetable with butter, three. It's safe to say that anything under seven steps would be okay. That means not eating foods like; vegetable oil, margarine, imitation crab (the word imitation should give it away), processed cheese slices, aspartame, store-bought yogurt, chicken nuggets, french fries, Powerade, and the list goes on.

2. Eat carbohydrates that are shaped like vegetables. Carbohydrates that aren't shaped like vegetables include breads, crackers, bagels, muffins, cakes, and pastries. (And no fair cutting your bread into the shape of a vegetable.)

3. Eat meat and fat. Real fat, like lard, butter, or coconut oil. (See item 1 for the definition of 'real.')

4. Don't eat legumes. Yes, I said it. Stop eating beans that hurt your gut. Beans, beans, the musical fruit, the more you eat, the more chance you'll have colitis and an irritable bowel.[13]

SLEEP:

Go to bed.

Sleep in a dark room without your iPad, YouTube videos, or flashing, blinking LEDs. For eight hours in a row. Sleep like it matters. I know some days it isn't possible due to babies, periods of insomnia or a regrettable late evening coffee but it's part of the unsecret formula. It won't make anyone money, because it's not gimmicky or fun. It's just called getting a good night's sleep to reset your cortisol levels. It will actually make fat go away.[14] Sleep.

BREATHE:

Breathe, and then breathe and squeeze out a smile. "Breathe" is the word I use to remind people that life should be fun. Remembering to breathe is like remembering to take your happy pill. The word "breathe" can be taken literally to mean 'take a deep breath' physically, but it has also come to signify taking a deep breath of life. Without some kind of passion in your life, all the other stuff is hard to manage. Breathing could mean meditating, resting, reading, hiking, or cooking a meal for friends. Whatever activity makes you feel at peace with yourself. Your health is the first to suffer when you don't have one damned fun breath in you.

MOVE:

1. Walk.

2. Move heavy things.

3. Sometimes run fast.

4. Stretch.

Any one of these will make you feel alive. All of these will stimulate your body to respond positively. Hire a trainer, find a friend, or just Google something that you might be interested in that will make you move.

That's it. The unsecret, unveiled.

You might still be fat even if you follow these four steps. Why? Because each time you overload your body with sugar, stress, fatigue, and inactivity, you wear down the mechanisms your body uses to maintain your ideal weight. Each time, it gets harder to fix the problem. The four pillars will bring you health, but they won't always bring you thinness and that's okay because who you are will always be more important than how you look.

Everyone can be an asshole when it comes to health. We judge and we compare. Finding your own health success is a personal journey that needs to come with earplugs from well-intentioned friends and family.

If this is a slice you are ready to pursue, then do it with vigor and an open mind. Do it with passion and a light heart. Taking this journey toward health can be a fabulous way to discover what makes you feel great. Getting outside, going on an adventure, racing, exploring, meditating, and just breathing are a tiny sample of ways to invigorate your desire to feel alive.

My Own Struggle

With thirty pounds to lose, it was hard for me to wear the trainer hat. I couldn't. Who would hire a trainer or speaker that knew the right answers but couldn't apply them to herself? There were many things I had to accept before I could restart my health slice:

- I was putting other people's needs ahead of mine.
- I was feeding my feelings.
- I had stopped caring about my appearance and my health.
- I was using my children as a shield to hide my body in photos.
- I was thinking about exercising, but fantasizing about sleeping.
- I had decided I would rather look like this than summon the energy and courage to get back to a better me.

No matter how I rationalized this weight gain, my delusion came to a grinding halt when I discovered that I needed therapy to buy a bathing suit. I was in a store dressing room when I texted Tina for help.

HEATHER: Tina, I'm at Walmart shopping for a bathing suit. This trumps all loathsome tasks to be completed at Walmart. I'll send pictures. No, no I won't. Probably never. Xoxo.

HEATHER: Where are you? I need you. I've just changed my priority list. Finishing the book is now secondary to looking less like a cow stuffed in a sausage skin. Vanity wins—intellectual success loses.

HEATHER: I'll just keep typing like you are there. Please make this mirror show me the "after" picture. It's like I'm covered in papier-mâché and underneath is the tautly shaped human I'm supposed to be.

TINA: I'm here for you. I was just eating the frosting off my kid's cupcakes. It would be so easy if our fat was *papier-mâché*. One bath and we would be skinny. Pasty, but skinny.

HEATHER: Ha ha. Why don't they make full-body bathing suits? Like a swimming pantsuit?

TINA: Why did we ever do away with the bathing dresses our great-grandmas wore? What the hell does Oprah swim in?

HEATHER: I don't know, gold? This is seriously the end of cookie-row eating.

Tina: I understand. We need to get rich so our fat doesn't matter.

HEATHER: WTF. I'm going to look into herbal magic. Here's a book title for you: *HOW TO BEAT FATCER*—like cancer, but fat.

TINA: Just do what every mom does, get a colorful cover-up and a giant hat.

HEATHER: Funny, I was just looking at hats.

TINA: Yep, get one that casts a shadow over your thighs.

HEATHER: Cowboy hat?

TINA: Yes, ten gallon.

HEATHER: I will need therapy tonight. Should we stop eating sugar?

TINA: I can't work without carbs, just so you know.

HEATHER: I understand. I can't go swimming without a body tarp.

It felt like I needed to sacrifice a hundred things in some other slice to dedicate enough time and energy to this slice. Years of raising a family and working had put my health slice on hold. My fitness level fell, and my weight climbed. I struggled with getting back on track, because I couldn't see how I was going to make it work. I felt angry that I would have to give up writing time or family time to carve out a slice of anti-*papier-mâché* time. I wanted to be ready, and I wanted to be successful because I couldn't face another season of bathing suit shopping. So I began.

I started with the EAT pillar. It's the one that gets the fastest results. Two months later, I added the MOVE pillar. After seven months, I had lost fifteen of the thirty pounds. I have another fifteen to go, but I'd be happy with ten. I work at the four pillars of health daily. When I get a normal amount of unbroken sleep, I lose weight. I work out in small amounts in our home gym, and I do it with the kids. My workouts aren't much longer than ten or fifteen minutes, but they keep me motivated and feeling strong. I follow a low carb eating program about 80 percent of the time, and I remember to plan a goal that fires up my passion for living.

I'm already feeling so much better. The health slice is one that needs attention, even if you can manage only one pillar. Eat, sleep, move, or breathe. Sometimes I rest on my own sense of entitlement. I work hard and take care of my family. Why shouldn't I enjoy a glass of wine and a slice of pie?

And that's the answer.

Of course we should be able to enjoy a slice of pie—just not the whole pie.

Just finished hiking the Grand Canyon, top to bottom and back to top in seven and a half hours. 1990. Photo by: Travis Edwards.

CHAPTER ELEVEN

* * *

Bonus Slice: Sex, Lies, and Leprechauns

Imagine signing up for a work-life balance seminar that included writing down your sex goals and sex action steps. My husband never wants to talk about our financial goals, but if I said, "Sweetie, we need to set some goals for our sex life," he would show up naked with a notebook and a pen tucked behind his ear.

Sex, a topic that used to be too private, too intimate to talk about, has recently seen an explosion in its availability and public consumption. Money problems, rocky marriages, parenting conflicts, and sex used to be topics kept behind closed doors. Each passing decade saw the unveiling of people's personal lives until sex was the only taboo left. Now commercials, articles, TV shows, and movies have brought Viagra, vaginal moisture cream, sex toys, and swinger parties into the open, brazenly naked for everyone to see. Sex is officially out of the closet, and personally, I don't want to stuff it back in. I like sex. It deserves its own slice in the life pie—a salacious wedge of banana cream.

Lies and Lists

Here's the sex interview every good tabloid magazine should have:

Q. Do all women fake orgasms?

A. Yes. Not all the time, but sometimes.

Q. Do women care that they don't reach orgasm?

A. Not always. If they want to have one, they will make sure to get one.

Q. Do all men think about other women or porn when they are having sex?

A. Yes. Not all the time, but sometimes, lots of times, perhaps most of the time.

Q. Does this matter?

A. No, because it's normal and unavoidable if a couple has been together for more than ten minutes.

Q. Should women tell men what they want?

A. Yes. They should tell them and then tell them again, because men never listen the first time. Even if they are told, "The man in the canoe is a gentle soul that can't be scrubbed or palmed like a basketball," sometimes they forget.

Q. Should a man show a woman how to handle his member and guide her in a way that makes it exciting and pleasing?

A. Yes, because men and women don't own the same equipment, and a few pointers on the bits that stick out could be helpful.

Q. Can a penis ever be too big?

A. Yes.

Q. Can a penis ever be too small?

A. Yes.

Q. Why don't women want to have sex when they get into bed at the end of the evening?

A. Before bed, my husband will say, "I'm going to bed." Then he will brush his teeth, take off his pants, and get into bed. Before I go to bed, I pack the kids' lunches, fill out the forms for school events, load the dishwasher, tidy the front door, throw a load of wash in, put the wet clothes in the dryer, prep the coffeemaker, wipe down the kitchen counters, turn off the lights in the basement, lock the doors, close the blinds, check on each of the kids, brush my teeth, go back downstairs because I forgot to turn on the dishwasher, come back upstairs, put on my pajamas, and crawl into bed. I would probably have sex at the end of the evening too - if all I had to do was take off my pants.

When I think of sex, I think of lust, romance, and passion. I think of hormones, tingling labia, and wanton abandon. These are the ideas that make up the sex slice for me. Sex is one of the few experiences that allows me to let go and lose myself in a moment of pleasure. I think about sex and I sigh, because it can be so damn good.

Yet for me, as for most women, this release means letting go not only of my inhibitions, but of my day-to-day realities. It means releasing the mind-numbing, soul-permeating to-do list that chatters around in my brain twenty-four hours a day—the list that helps me prioritize tasks and prepare for the coming week, day, minute, and minutiae of my life. Forget hormones and getting old and fatness and self-esteem—the list is what leaves me completely devoid of the desire to spontaneously jump on my partner and ride that train into the station. The list and its complicated, intertwined branches makes me feel like some days, sex is just one more thing to get done.

Good sex takes effort. It requires a decision to relax and let go. It is my choice to enjoy sex, and if the laundry and the grocery shopping are done, it ensures my thoughts are more on being a lover and less about clutter. There are three things we do regularly to work on this slice. First, we plan to have sex. We enter an agreed upon 'appointment time' in our shared online calendar. Boring? Yes. But it's the only way we end up with this time together. Second, I write everything down that I have to do that's rolling around in my head *before* we roll around in the proverbial hay – and I mean everything. I have two expired passports that need renewing for the kids, this is not a thought I want popping into my head while I'm trying to enjoy myself. And third, I ask a very simple question to my husband, "Any special requests?" Then I give a list of options that might get both of us in the mood. It works. Sometimes we don't even need all three steps and we have spontaneous-we aren't married with kids, sex – go figure.

Leprechauns

When we first met, my husband told me his favorite holiday was Halloween. Although I don't technically consider that a holiday, I was happy to learn that he's comfortable with dress-up, role playing, and chocolate. On a cold day in March, seven years into our marriage and three children later, I got a call from Mark on his way home from work.

"Hey babe, I'm going to be a bit late getting home. I'm getting my costume together."

I was cradling the phone with our five-month-old on my hip and the other two kids squalling in the background. "It's March. I know you like Halloween, but really, honey? The kids are sick, and I could use a break here."

"No, my costume for St. Paddy's Day."

"What?" In a nanosecond, four thoughts ran through my head:

You're going out for St. Patrick's Day?

I have to watch our virus-laden children while you drink green beer?

A costume? Isn't Halloween enough for you?

What part of our wedding vows included binge drinking dressed as a leprechaun?

I didn't say any of these things, because I wasn't up for the debate. Nagging my husband about this ritual was about as successful as talking to my kids about doing their own laundry. I felt deflated just thinking about it.

"That's nice, honey."

Mark arrived home giddy and proceeded to open his bags of goodies from the Salvation Army and the dollar store. He was staring in the mirror as he grabbed items from the bags.

"Hon, which hat seems more leprechauny?"

"The one with the sideburns attached."

"Check out these shoes. Could they be any more Irish?" He held up his new footwear for me to see.

"Don't you feel bad buying these things for a costume when poor people might need them for, I don't know, a job interview?"

"No. Because black leather shoes with giant silver buckles wouldn't get you hired."

"Right."

I continued to help him select his best outfit, all the while wondering whether it occurred to him that his anticipated night of small-green-man fun fell on spring break. He would be out, and I would be imprisoned with the kids, the youngest still attached to my nipple. I realized that what I wanted to say would make me seem like the mad wife, the endless downer, the no-fun ball and chain. But my emotional brain was screaming, *ARE YOU INSANE? How could you think it's your turn for another get-out-of-the-house day? It's my turn, and I'm running out the door and leaving you here with the kids, the mess, the laundry, the meals, and the damn box of fishy crackers they've thrown like confetti on the carpet.*

On St. Patrick's Day, Mark made sure I got to sleep in, cooked me breakfast, and spent the day entertaining the kids. If these were part of the trade-off, maybe it wouldn't be so bad. He headed out in the early evening with bits of costume and his best Irish intentions. As the door clicked closed, I mentally planned my evening. Which row of cookies would I eat? What Disney movie could I put on repeatedly for the kids? I scanned the movie list and checked the treat cupboard. Oreos and Ariel, carbs and fantasy, sugar and dreams. I would survive. Maybe.

At eight o'clock I received a text from my husband:

I really love u.

Uh-oh. What had happened? We'd been married long enough that drunk texting was a thing of the past. I wondered whether he had stumbled on a taut hottie with an Irish lilt. He's not a flirty-guy so this didn't seem likely. I mean, it was eight o'clock—what kind of trouble could he get into before midnight? An unsolicited text this early made me nervous. Then my phone rang.

"Hello, honey." I tried not to sound anxious.

"I mish you. I'm comin' 'ome. I really, really love being wish you, babe. I hidda turning point in my life. The bar whass filled with univershity shtudents." He hiccupped. "Oh, I shtopped at the sex shtore on the way home. I love you."

"Really? Are you okay? Did you get in a fight? I love you too. What's going on? It's eight thirty. Seriously, you have the hiccups? What sex store?"

Mark went on to tell me that drinking beer with a bunch of college students wasn't where he wanted to be. My guess was that he wanted to be home in his king-sized bed with his stable, loving wife who made sure there were eggs on the stove and coffee in the pot in the morning.

Of course, there was the matter of the sex store. Going to the sex store was not new for us. The arrival of our three babies in quick succession meant that AA batteries were not just for the kids' toys anymore. We had talked about adding a few upgrades to our arsenal of love paraphernalia, but I never imagined that in a drunken stupor, dressed as a leprechaun, Mark would be thinking of me. In his hat and beard, green knickers, long socks, silver-buckled shoes, and corncob pipe, he went shopping for the "Rabbit," the "Dolphin," and something called the "Thorgasm" for his wife.

When Mark stumbled through the door with a big grin and fake sideburns, I couldn't help but laugh. In that moment I could have chosen to be angry. I could have counted up all the things I had to do while he was out, but I didn't. I made a conscious decision to be happy. Seeing him standing in the doorway holding a bag of sex toys reminded me that my husband is a fun, thoughtful, caring guy who loves spending time with me, be it for a coffee, a bike ride, or sex. When we are together, we talk about our goals and our kids and current events. Our relationship lets me feel safe and confident that he's buying these toys because he wants to please me and keep the joy in our sex. If intimacy is the only thing that separates a marriage from friendship, then it's essential to staying together as a couple. It's the fun in our sex that makes it okay to pretend that I am having my way with a magical green man who is promising me a pot of gold at the end of a vibrating rainbow.

Fu*kerware Parties

Men think about sex more than women, but women talk about sex more than men.[16] Women talk about it in coffee shops, during bike rides, and at play dates. We are shockingly real and honest about our problems and triumphs. Men would shiver if they heard us.

My last neighbor, a mother of three married to an Amish-born husband, recently approached me at the end of my driveway to chat. She got right to the point.

"Hey, Heather, I've started my own business, and I wonder if you'd be interested in an introductory party at my house." Immediately I thought, *Run now, before the word 'Tupperware' comes out of her mouth*, but I had nowhere to hide. Being a good neighbor, I just stood there with a smile on my face, mentally preparing my escape. She said, "I'm starting a Passion Party business—you know, in-home parties to sell sex toys. I'm having a party in two weeks. Would you be interested in coming?"

My inside voice was running amok. *Oh my God, sex toys made by the Amish? Hand-carved wooden dildos and organic, farm-fresh lubricants? No wonder they don't need electricity.*

Instead I stammered, "Uh, oh, wow. I didn't think you were going to say that. Um, sure. Do I need to bring anything?"

"No, I'll have everything we need. It will be fun!"

"Yes. I'm sure it will be." I waved and walked back toward my house, wondering what I would wear to a fu*kerware party.

Sex toy parties, sex conventions, and magazine articles depicting the best way to reach orgasm have opened the vault-door to people's intimate lives. For some, this openness is a horrible statement on society; for others, it's a relief. One thing is for certain: this newfound willingness to talk about sex means that it's one more area in which we are comparing ourselves to others. People aren't afraid to tell you when their sex lives are good or bad, and this makes it tough to navigate your own personal slice of happy sex.

All of this openness is great unless your sexual adventures don't match the normal spectrum of the average person. Most people will admit to sex in different places, sex when someone might catch them, oral sex, sex toys, maybe even a few sexy photos. But sneak in a few questions about anal sex, threesomes, or bondage, and watch people's faces contort as they find a reason to excuse themselves to another area of the party. It's easy to know your tastes are unconventional if the mention of nipple clamps quiets the room. But just because something is not for you doesn't mean it's abnormal. Sexual appetite is as unique as the people enjoying their sex slice.

I think sex should be fun. I admire anyone who has the courage to try something exciting or new for them. Times are changing. According to a report aired on ABC's *20/20* in 2005, nearly four million North Americans are engaged in a swinging lifestyle.[16] 'Swingers' are consenting adults who engage in multiple-partner sex swapping. It can be as simple as exchanging partners with another couple or as complex as a whole bunch of people attending a planned pheromone-sniffing party. I find this fascinating.

Right now a movement that involves spouse swapping is being coordinated over Twitter and Facebook. Can you imagine the comments? As I scoured the websites for more info, I inwardly asked myself, *Would this work? Would I be okay with my husband having sex with someone at a party while I enjoyed another man teasing my furry furnace?*

I couldn't resist imagining this scenario in my head. I closed my eyes and conjured an image of my husband and me walking up the steps to a pre-determined love shack.

"Did you bring the invitation?" I ask my husband.

"Yes, it's right here."

I glance down at the little card in his hand.

Avoid the pitfalls of boredom and infidelity in your marriage by having a more open sexual relationship! Come to our next Meet and Greet, Hang and Bang and see if it's for you! Just ring the bell and use the code word "lube."

I press my finger on the button at the side of the door.

Ding dong.

"Honey, did you bring the breath mints? Do you think the lights will be dim enough? My skin is dry, oh lord, I wish I had a tan. Do you think they use Febreze? I hate that smell." Then I glance down and see my muffin top, and I think, *Am I really going to just take my pants off? Should I have brought a robe? Or a hostess gift? Do you bring a hostess gift to an orgy?*

That's when I run away. I don't get past ringing the doorbell. Even in my fantasy, meeting other people to have sex with just seems awkward. It's outside my comfort zone, but for four million people, this is normal. Perhaps this is the next evolution—a couple that is happy to sample other people's sex slice of the pie while still staying married to their favorite slice.

Proponents of this lifestyle claim that it's natural to want to have sex with other people. For some, it's an option that's better than cheating. Avoid infidelity by having group sex—hmm.

According to the award-winning book *Sex at Dawn,* having multiple sex partners was the norm for our pre-agricultural ancestors. Coauthors Christopher Ryan and Cacilda Jethá took an in-depth look at the historical sex lives of 'cave dwellers.' In this nonfiction read, far more titillating than *Fifty Shades of Grey,* they conclude that as a species, we were never supposed to have just one sexual partner, but a host of them. Why did we start out as a swingers in the first place and what led us to the current trend of monogamy?

The answer, according to *Sex at Dawn,* stems from a time before there was scarcity and brings forward the "nature versus nurture" debate. Our nature is that both men and women have a sexual appetite for multiple sex partners. This desire gave children a greater chance of survival. The authors argue that human beings evolved in egalitarian hunter-gatherer groups in which sexual interaction was a shared resource, much like food, child care, and group defense. Simply put, they shared sex within the tribe, like a giant swinger party all the time. The theory is that if we all made the baby, then we would all share in caring for the baby, including finding food, protecting it, and ensuring that the baby grew up to be a functioning part of the tribe.

Culturally, marriage and long-term relationships are the norm, but when did the switch occur? The dawn of agriculture changed everything. Once we learned how to farm and stopped being nomadic, we had the potential to have more children with greater survival rates. Food became more plentiful, land ownership was more coveted, and societies became patriarchal. Patriarchy was and is about power and ownership, with women being another type of possession. These possessions, in turn, needed to be protected. Human instinct was to have multiple sex partners, but the new style of living created a desire for loyalty and thus monogamy.[17]

Ten thousand years later, we are still debating what is right. What is the right way to be married? What is the right way to communicate? What is the right way to have sex? I think the answer is simple. What is right is what works for you and your partner. It's important that you both agree on the type of relationship you are willing to enter and what the boundaries of that relationship are going to be. Your sex slice may look wildly different than mine. Monogamous, swinger, nipple clamper—whatever works for you as a couple is what will make it last.

A Movie and Some Porn-Corn

Sex is out there for public consumption: TV, movies, free online porn—it's everywhere. I can't imagine entering my teens in a world filled with vast amounts of online hardcore porn. My kids won't be stumbling on a dirty magazine, but instead wandering into a world where a misplaced click leads to a pop-up of a Brazilian-waxed, breast-implanted, aspiring female actress. If the only sex education you got was from porn, it would be normal to assume that every man is carrying a package the size of a cucumber and that women have pert twenty-year-old boobs and vaginas made for storing small appliances. But if you are more like the average person, and pornography wasn't your primary sex education resource, you were probably exposed to enough ideas to make an informed choice about what appeals to you.

When I see a flash of porn, for those few seconds I feel excited, intrigued, and googly-eyed. I can't believe that people get paid to do this. But then if I'm exposed to it a bit longer—like, oh, twenty seconds—I feel disconnected. The camera angles, the lights, the giant erections, the endless pounding and grunting—everything is exaggerated and intensified until it feels like a cartoon in which larger-than-life Kens and Barbies prance around singing and dancing in the bedroom, completely naked, with glistening hoohahs and taut wieners. They hop and they hum, they grunt and they groan, and at the culmination of the routine they have a giant orgy on the central stage at the princess palace. Maybe porn is the Disneyland of sex?

I think the entertainment industry has placed an extraordinary burden on a married couple's sex life. The expectations for a highly varied, romantic, deeply fulfilling sex life are too high. At some point, most marriages suffer from boredom, complacency, and routine. This happens with sex too. The sexual lust that you have at the beginning of a relationship fades. The natural chemicals that make it feel so magical and great at the start don't hang around forever. A common lament from couples in long-term relationships is, "I don't know where the sexual lust went." No one does. The early relationship love-lust and euphoria can never be recaptured at the same intensity as when you first met. This is just part of life.

Now more than ever, the entertainment industry is filling the gap. At the extreme end of the spectrum, there is unlimited free porn available to anyone with an internet connection but on the other side of the chasm there is a more subtle way entertainment is bridging the distance between reality and fantasy. They are creating entertainment that meets two distinct desires: action dramas with sexual conquests, and romantic fantasies with emotional connections. Very few men want to watch a ninety-minute romantic comedy in which the final scene is a couple having missionary sex under the covers with the lights off. Conversely, most women are less intrigued by blood-spurting shoot-'em-ups in which the bad guy is banging a smoking hot babe. The media give women emotionally connected chick flicks, and they give men a healthy dose of testosterone-laced, fast-action dramas in which someone gets laid. The industry fills a gap between what we dream our lives will be like and what they are really like. Men get married because they *hope* they will have more sex, not less, and women get married so they can feel secure enough to stop shaving.

Lies and the Genome

"Hey, Tina, did I ever tell you that Victoria's husband cheated on her and that's why they divorced?"

"No kidding?"

"Yeah. She was away on a business trip, and when she came home, she noticed that the spare bedroom looked different."

"Ugh, I hate when we notice everything. It makes my stomach hurt just thinking about this."

"Right. So she checked the bed, and of course the sheets weren't the way she left them and the cover was spread right to the top instead of being turned down."

"Oh, man, that sucks. Did she actually catch them, or was she basing it on an assumption?"

"No, she asked him if he slept in the bed, and he said he wasn't feeling good and didn't want to sleep in their bed in case he was sick."

"Uh-huh, sounds unlikely."

"Exactly. So she checked the bed carefully and found long blonde hair strands. She's a dark brunette."

"She used the hair to tell him she knew?"

"No, she sent it away for DNA testing!"

"Seriously? That's brilliant. Did she find out whose hair it was?" Tina sounded more than impressed with Victoria's actions.

"No, but the lab report said there was only a one in 397-million chance it was hers."

"Why do men always want to have sex with someone else?" Tina asked.

I nodded my head at the other end of the phone in agreement. "Oh, lord, because it's fun, it's exciting, it's new—who knows. I know lots of women do the same."

"Yeah, but what does it take to keep the sex alive?" Tina asked, even though she'd been married longer than I had.

"I don't know, this is a baffling question because even when it's good it doesn't seem to matter."

"Hey, ask the girls while you're in Muskoka—see if they have any secrets we could borrow."

The next day I was heading out of town for our annual girls' weekend. Tina wouldn't be able to make it, but she suggested that I take our dilemma to the small group of ladies we meet with once a year in order to escape our kids, cooking, and laundry while we drink wine and pamper ourselves.

"I will. I wish you were coming."

"Me too."

Vibrating Muskoka Chairs

The girls' weekend is like any weekend where women get away from the daily tasks that keep us from, well, having fun. We drink wine, eat delectable nibbles, ride our bikes, hug, and talk.

"All right, ladies! I brought the trashy magazines. There's *People*, *Us*, and of course, the *National Enquirer*. Everyone got their drink?" Cailee demanded more than questioned. I call her Crazy Cailee, because she's a to-the-limit kind of girl. She runs ultramarathons and is a national hero in the adventure-racing world. She doesn't do anything half-assed.

"OH MY GOD!" Cailee yelled as she flipped through her *People* magazine.

"What?" Patricia asked. Patricia is quite possibly the sanest of our bunch, but she is also not currently married or time-scarred by raising children.

"Did you see that Ryan Phillipe cheated on Reese Witherspoon with the BABYSITTER?!"

We all laughed. "Yes, Cailee, we heard. Where have you been?"

"But this is crazy! What the hell is wrong with this guy? He has sex with the babysitter and they have two kids?"

That's when I remembered what Tina and I were talking about. "Ladies!" I interrupted. "I need some help—I need some ideas."

As we all refilled our glasses, I asked for their help. "I need, like, three or four things that you do to make sex fun."

"Why? Are you having boring sex?" Elise asked. "Your husband is so hot. I'll have sex with him if you need a break." We all laughed. Elise knew that Mark and I have a good sex life, but it was nice to know she appreciated looking at my husband like I do.

"No, but I was talking to Tina, and we were trying to come up with a list of ideas to keep our husbands from canoodling the babysitter or the cleaning lady or anyone else who doesn't wear our underwear."

Anika was the first to pipe up. "Okay, I have one: control. Like, role play scenarios—doctor and patient, teacher and student..."

Before she finished her sentence, I yelled out, "Or massage therapist and client?"

"Ha! Is that yours?" Patricia chirped.

"Yes, maybe—in my mind. I pretend my hubby is my massage therapist, and as he starts rubbing me, he lets his fingers kind of slip around to tickle my love button and then accidentally uses his power wand to give me a deep-tissue massage—like it's part of the service, you know?"

"Ha! Have you told him this?" Cailee asked incredulously.

"Are you kidding? If I told him that, he'd think every time I went to the naturopathic clinic, the word 'massage' was code for 'penetration.'"

"True. Or maybe he would give you more massages if you told him your fantasy." Elise used some nice logic to advance the cause.

"Pah! If I told my husband that, I would never get the actual massage. He would be more like a chiropractor and just step into the treatment room for a quick adjustment." We giggled as we drank our pinot grigio and enjoyed some chocolate-covered almonds.

"Okay, so giving up control and having a bit of fantasy—these are good, but I need more," I said. "I want to have a full repertoire to keep it fresh." We got giddier as we talked, but it gave us all a chance to unwind.

Cailee piped up again with a bit less vigor. "I would love it if my husband told me exactly how he wanted it, where I should focus my efforts. You girls know how I love a goal. It would make everything easier and more—I don't know—exciting. If I could let go of control and have him direct me, it would mean the other side of my brain wouldn't be trying to figure out what to make for dinner." Silent nods as we all agreed that a chattier husband would go a long way in adding some spice.

As we hashed out a few more ideas, I threw out the next thought in my head. "Porn?"

I'd hit a nerve, because it seemed I was not the only one who didn't quite know what to make of our generation being smothered in porn. Since no one was saying anything, I started. "It can be good, you know. I don't mind watching it with my husband, but if he watches it alone, it makes me crazy, like Angela Bassett in *Waiting to Exhale,* throw-his-clothes-on-the-front-lawn crazy."

"ARGHHH." It was a collective growl. It was like we'd all experienced the heart-breaking feeling of knowing that our husbands watch porn, glance at porn, see porn in some form—and that form is not us.

"Okay. Let's take porn off the list. It's just going to make everyone angry."

"Agreed," said Elise. "What about kissing? I know it sounds lame, but oh, think back to those first kisses. The ones that make you stop in your tracks and melt on the spot." This time there was a collective "Ah." Elise's suggestion made us all pause as we thought back to those awesome first kisses and how they liquefied our insides.

"Oh, I agree." I was totally on board with this suggestion. "Kisses are not lame. We need to bring them back into marriages. Not just a quick peck, but the full metal jacket of kissing—the soft-hard, mix it up, grab-me-by-the-head kissing."

"Okay, kissing, and maybe romance?" Patricia suggested.

I was the first to belt out a laugh, but we all found this funny. Patricia was recently divorced, so in her world of new dates, the opportunity for romance still existed.

"You're funny. What the hell is romance? I just want my husband not to confuse manners with romance. Having a shower before sex isn't romantic, it's good manners. Wearing something nice out to dinner isn't romantic, it's good manners," I clarified.

"Agreed. Romance to me is more like doing something thoughtful without being asked." Cailee was well into her fourth glass, and the word "something" came out like "sumsing."

As the thought of romance hit my brain and the wine loosened my tongue, I yelled to the air, "Honey, romance me and clean out my car!" I continued as if my husband was in the other room and could hear my plea. "While you're polishing your man truck like it's a Fabergé egg, can you please clean out my car? It's not even *my* car, it's the family car. Could you just empty the kid garbage from my car?" I continued to send my wine-induced war cry out to the northern stars. "Get the petrified french fries, sippy cups, half-eaten granola bars, coffee cups, receipts, pens, papers, skipping ropes, the eighty thousand small toys, and the few million crumbs from every car trip we've ever taken and just put them in the trash? Thanks, babe." I finished my tirade with a final yell: "AND THEN WE CAN HAVE SEX ALL NIGHT"

We all laughed, not because it was so funny, but because we were drunk and maybe, just maybe, this was what counted for romance ten years into a marriage.

The Sex Slice

Sex is toughest on a couple when their 'normals' are too far apart. Sex-every-day guy is not going to work with once-a-month-sex woman. Multiple-sex-partner person is not going to work with monogamous-sex spouse. We are all happy when we have intimacy that pleases us, but how do couples figure it out year after year? Words like 'trust' and 'fun' are a good place to start. Remembering to like each other and choosing to see the 'sexy' in your partner takes practice. Taking little steps—like kissing more, talking about sex, or maybe acquiring a few toys—can go a long way toward filling this slice. We can all use a bit of imagination to shake up our sex routines— you just need to pick the spice that will fix up this slice.

There is only one kind of pie I think about when I think of the sex slice: the all-pleasing, wonderful banana cream pie, perhaps with some extra whipped cream, bigger bananas, or more creamy custard—whatever your palate desires. Have a little taste and see if it's for you and your partner. I truly hope sex only gets better each time I have this deliciously carnal slice of happy.

Mark (husband), Scott Morrison, Greg Williams, and Drew Dancey heading out for St. Paddy's day 2011.

CHAPTER TWELVE

* * *

Wealth: Wait! Don't Sell That Kidney Yet

Money.

It has been said that *money is the root of all evil*, but it *doesn't grow on trees*, and *money makes money*, but you shouldn't get all wrapped up in it because *money isn't everything*. Don't be foolish or *you and your money will be soon parted*, even though *the best things in life are free*. I guess it goes without saying, *you can't take it with you when you die*.

It's hard to imagine that a piece of paper can cause so much distress or joy, and that money, the symbol of our commerce, controls most of our lives. Money is tricky because it's not an actual thing—it's a placeholder for a thing. Paper money was created to act as an IOU for the value of a good that was too cumbersome to move. Now money is worth something only if we follow the rules of trading paper for goods. In times of strife, people will always need food, water, and shelter, but pieces of paper will have little or no value. Only in a world filled with order can money exist. I struggle with this concept, because it appears the bulk of North Americans live one paycheck above chaos. Piles of money, loads of land, and batches of gold bullion will always be part of the imagery of wealth, but is there more to the wealth slice than dollar signs?

Should the definition of wealth include having abundance in body, mind, and spirit as well as tangible assets? Would a monk who owned almost nothing in the physical realm but possessed powerful mental and spiritual connections still be considered wealthy outside of the monastery? A monk might say yes, but someone who had a penchant for heated car seats might disagree. What is enough for one person may not be nearly enough for another, and this is why defining the wealth slice can be elusive.

"Heather, truth or dare?"

"Truth."

"Okay, would you sell a kidney for money?"

"NO! Never. Are you kidding me? Wait. How much money?"

Is there a price so great that I could be persuaded to sell one of my vital organs? Two million dollars? Less? More? What if I died during the surgery and my kids didn't have a mommy because I thought this would be the answer, the ticket to financial freedom?

Selling a kidney in North America is against the law, but this hasn't stopped people from trying. One attempt on eBay resulted in the ad being pulled in the middle of a bidding war.[18] Some people need kidneys, and some people need money. When a person's life is at stake, people will trade every dime they own to have their health back. What good is wealth if you need a kidney to live? And what good is an extra kidney if you have so little wealth you can't live? Wealth is a shifty word that blurs the line between surviving and thriving. Most people want more of it and some people will do almost anything to get it.

What Is Enough?

It's clear that we all have a money comfort zone—some amount that is sufficient to satisfy our needs and at least some of our wants. If wealth didn't include tangible assets like money or property, this chapter would be called "Warm, Fuzzy Emotions" or "I Live with My Parents." But how much is enough?

I called Tina at ten o'clock Monday morning with a desire to solve my wealth problem.

"Tina, I want to talk about being poor."

"Why?"

"Because I think it might be easier."

"To be poor?"

"Yes."

"Well, don't let anyone pushing a grocery cart in the alley hear you say that."

"I know. I sound ridiculous and spoiled, but I wonder why we try so hard to get ahead. I never get anywhere."

"I think trying to get ahead is programmed into our DNA," Tina suggested.

I applied her theory to my present state of mind. "You mean once we get past struggling to survive, we push on and struggle to take a vacation?"

"Yes, and pay the bills, invest for the future, try not to go bankrupt—you know, what every middle-class family struggles with."

"It seems pointless. When I have a tiny bit of extra money, it's eaten up in taxes or unexpected expenses. That makes me wonder if the struggle is worth it."

"What do you mean?" Tina questioned.

"If every day my job was to find clean water, get some food, and fix my hut, I would at least know what my purpose was. How can I pursue getting ahead when I live in a place where my purpose is obscured by remembering whether garbage day is Tuesday because Monday was a holiday?" I explained.

"I know. Our problems are like a gnat on an elephant compared to what other people face, but we still have to find solutions, because this is *our* reality. Summer break is about ten seconds away, and I have no idea what I'm going to do with my kids. They aren't old enough to be home alone, and summer camp costs a fortune. I can't afford not to work, but I can't afford to send them somewhere."

"Right. Not rich enough to throw money at it, not poor enough to qualify for any support." I thought about all the decisions I struggle with that a person with no money would wish they had the luxury to consider. "It's like when we go on a vacation, I start trading sanity for money. I book cheaper connecting flights to save a few bucks, and end up wondering how many plane transfers we can survive with three kids in tow."

"Uh-huh. Or you drive there and try not to commit family vacation, car suicide." I laughed at the truth of Tina's statement as I tried to summarize my dilemma.

"I want less and more at the same time—less stress and more money, less stuff and more time. I'm chronically over informed with a million choices and underfunded to choose what I think is right."

"Maybe if we just tried harder, we would be rich?" Tina questioned.

"Maybe if we just stopped trying so hard, we would be happy," I retorted.

When I listen to people with lots of money complain, I hear the same phrase repeated: "It's so hard to find good help." Cleaning staff, pool people, gardeners, accountants, lawyers, and personal assistants all seem to be part of managing the pesky annoyances of being wealthy. I don't have enough money to hire any help, so instead I complain about trying to get ahead. Further down the line are people complaining about not having enough money to buy food or secure housing. Take this to its lowest level, and you find people living in poverty, struggling to survive. Wealth is relative, and as with any other slice of the life pie, perspective will quickly remind you that having enough is an okay place to be.

When Is It Enough?

Is it okay to say that I have enough when I've met the basics of Maslow's hierarchy of needs:water, food, shelter, and clothing? To me this feels like the definition of surviving. I want more than survival. Most people want more than the bare necessities. What is the answer for the middle class, the people who appear to have it all but are only one or two paychecks away from not having anything? Where was Maslow when an iPhone somehow became essential?

Budget experts talk about defining your needs and wants. When you don't have enough money, your needs are never being fully met. At the other end of the spectrum, when money is abundant, wants and needs are barely differentiated. If you need it, you buy it. If you want it, you buy it. When you exist in the middle, where you have more than some and less than others, the line between a want and a need is fuzzy and ill-defined.

Lower middle class, middle class, or upper middle class—the middles struggle to find the answer daily. The members of this large part of society carry the burden of paying sizable taxes, insurance premiums, and licensing fees and use their expendable income to support the economy. Still, getting ahead feels like running on a hamster wheel attached to a treadmill in a wind tunnel.

As income levels continue to decline or stagnate for plenty of the population, costs continue to rise. There is a burgeoning gap between the wealthy elite and the middle class. No matter what dollar value you assign to the middle class, they are slowly being crushed by expenses that can't be clearly defined as needs or wants. There is a growing list of budget oddities that have become part of a giant money, decision-making flow-chart.

I struggle with budget oddities all the time. Look at the Internet – in my opinion it has moved from being a fun, useful tool to an essential part of living. One could still debate if we need the Internet, but my answer is yes. The budget question then becomes, how much? How much Internet, download capability, does one need? A capped amount or unlimited? Should my kids be able to use it to research school work, learn math or download games? It's just part of the decision making flow chart that arises daily.

What about snow tires? You may not live in a winter climate but here in Canada and many Northern States there is a lot of snow. Without snow tires there are days when neither my husband or I could get to work – is this okay? If the answer to that question is yes, then I would have to qualify the answer with another question. How many days would be acceptable to miss? This winter alone, without snow tires we would be well into twelve days or more of missed work, that's a lot of lost time and money. If we do have snow tires, should my husband buy the equipment to change them or should we pay a garage to service them? These are all easy questions but each one involves another line item on the budget.

Insurance is another on of those budget oddities. Do you need car insurance? Yes. Should you pay a lower monthly premium but accept a higher deductible? I don't know. What about disability insurance if you run your own business? If you couldn't work due to an illness or major injury could you still get by? The list goes on, is a gym membership worth the price of your health if it means you will pay less in health care costs? Should you invest in extended warranties if you suspect you won't be able to replace the item if it breaks? These are just a few examples of the life long decisions we make when money is not scarce but also not unlimited. Wants versus needs becomes an odd question when you live in the middle.

In my budget I have a heading called 'sanity items.'

The sanity branch has items that on the surface may seem like a complete waste of money, but support the bigger picture of staying sane. I would put visiting the McDonald's drive-through during a long car trip with the kids, high on the sanity branch. Clear storage bins, extra phone chargers, Netflix rentals, iPhone apps, and air conditioning during allergy season are all items that cost money, but keep me sane. Having clear storage bins saves me time when I'm trying to locate a seasonal item—if I can't find it; I end up buying a new one. Netflix is an obvious money saver when the cost of going out to the movies is prohibitive, but we still want to enjoy a night of entertainment with the kids. Using the air conditioning in the fall, even when the outdoor temperature is cool, means less money spent on allergy medications and less lost time from work. None of these items are needs, but they are also not wants. They fall in the space between people's basic needs for survival and Oprah's shoe closet.

Some days, sticking to a budget makes me feel like I'm never free. Some days I don't to think about the decision flow chart, I just want to spend some damn money. This is probably why I am not rich.

What are my needs and what are my wants? Buy mortgage life insurance or use that money for investments? Buy a gym membership or save the coin and go for a walk? Update my business website for better traffic or go to more personal networking meetings? Invest in my kids' future or my own? Shop organic? Buy snow tires? The list is endless, and the risk versus reward is hard to calculate. There is enough information out there to clog up my brain forever. The decision-making flowchart can become so overwhelming that I'd rather put it in the shredder than hear about one more way I should be saving or investing my tiny bit of money. Whatever happened to stuffing it under the mattress? When you are over-informed and underfunded, it becomes clear how making the wrong money decision can lead to consequences that could be pivotal to enjoying your wealth slice. The middle class struggles with the definition of enough, because we aren't poor and we aren't rich—we are squeezed.

This squeezing creates so much pressure that it takes away from finding our happy slice of wealth. There are only two scenarios in which being squeezed fades from my mind. There are days when the pressure of earning money leaves my head because I am enjoying a day at the beach with the kids or relaxing with my husband to watch a movie. I am able to compartmentalize the squeeze because I am focused on something else.

The other time the squeeze fades for me is when I have enough. Enough doesn't feel like a squeeze; it feels like wearing comfortable pants and taking a nap. For me, enough is when I'm not actively seeking more. It feels like I can breathe. I know this because I've had enough before, and it felt like

I was full. Money-full. I wasn't scraping together enough money to pay a bill. I wasn't moving money from one account to another. I wasn't elated to find twenty dollars in my winter coat pocket. (Okay, I'm always elated to find a surprise twenty-dollar bill.) Not being squeezed made me feel secure. For me, that was enough.

Right now, enough seems like a distant friend. There is constant pressure on the decision-making chart, and I am regularly weighing the options of spending on the items that will protect our current wealth like insurance or grow our wealth like an investment in my business. With all these thoughts, I decided to seek advice from someone who has money.

"I need a money personal trainer," I blurted out one day while I was training one of my more affluent clients.

"I'll give you my guy's name. He handles all of our investments." I knew Nathan meant well, but Nathan has bundles of money, and he thinks everyone else does too.

"Thanks, but I'm not looking for an investment adviser—I'm looking for someone to kick my ass with our budget. You know, someone who will tell me to stop buying things on iTunes and tell my husband that fishing trips aren't free just because he brings home a fish."

"Oh, you just need a budget. I assumed you already had one. They're pretty simple to come up with. You just track what you spend for a month, add in all the monthly fixed expenses, and subtract it from your income. Then you get a total—over or under."

He must have forgotten that I managed a business and my household and that I didn't just open my first bank account. His money smugness came from never having been without it.

"Right. I know. Track everything, file everything—I get it. I just have a hard time doing it."

"Why? It's not that tough. There are a ton of free programs online—just pick one and follow the steps."

Ha! I wanted to punch him because he didn't see the irony of hiring a personal trainer to get his body in shape when he could just *download a program online* – for free. "Thanks, I will."

I was lying. I wouldn't go online and download a budget program, because they don't work—unless you use them. It's like buying the MegaClimber Crosstrainer 2000, putting it in your bedroom, and then walking by it every day wishing it would make you thinner. Exercise equipment in people's bedrooms that reminds them they are still overweight is the same as a budget program with pop-up directives to remind me that I still don't have any money. I have tried to budget, and I have mostly failed. I say "mostly" because although my wealth slice isn't a mouth-popping pecan pie baked to perfection, it's also not an undercooked, ill-formed blueberry pie, all sloppy and running off the plate. It's somewhere in the middle.

From the time I graduated from university, I've run my own business. Anyone who has managed his or her own business knows that laying out a typical budget is trying at best, and at worst it makes you want to throw your computer across the room. Hiring a personal money trainer to enforce habitual money management skills is no different than clients hiring me to help them learn the habits of exercising and eating right. My lack of a concrete budget or financial plan is the giant elephant in the room. I stare at it and hope that it will sort itself out and not crap all over my future.

My wealth research has uncovered three common themes in the world of wealth management:

1. Live below your means.

2. Save.

3. Be content.

Three logical, simple concepts, and yet two parts are in direct conflict with the themes of wealth creation. Wealth creation is based on these three ideas:

1. Live below your means.

2. Invest.

3. Seek opportunity.

While living below your means is common to both concepts, the other items in the first list require the opposite actions of the second list. Being content with what you already have and saving any gains amounts to wealth protection. Wealth protection could be linked to the innate primal response of standing your ground and fighting for what you own instead of fleeing. On the other hand, creating wealth requires investing instead of saving and comes with a feeling of discontent with your current position. Creating wealth means seeking out growth opportunities, or the primal instinct to seek new resources, and perhaps gain greater abundance.

It seems we are hard wired to want to widen the gap between "survival" and "enough." Our culture wants a safety net, and it wants it to be made of money. For me to follow the advice of a person who lives frugally and squirrels away money is also to choose to stay where I am. I have always felt that I'm a runner, not a hider. It's hard for me to follow the path of saving and safety versus the path of exploration and spending. The happy in my wealth slice comes from seeking opportunities to increase my wealth instead of protecting it. This is the million-dollar question for the "middles;" how do you find your slice of happy in wealth when you are programmed to both protect what you have and strive to get ahead?

Manifesting Wealth

I used to have money. It flowed like Guinness beer at an Irish pub on a Friday night. When it ran low, I just turned on the work tap and made more. It was fantastic freedom: make money, spend money. Oh, happy, happy money.

"Road trip!" I shouted to my teammates. I was heavily into adventure racing, a multidisciplinary sport that requires lots of gear. My Santa wish list was filled with words like "Prusix-cords," "Gore-Tex," "carbon fiber," and my favorite, "multi-tool."

"Awesome—where are we going?" Gordo asked.

"Road trip to REI!" I yelled as visions of the giant outdoor rec store filled my head.

"That's not a road trip, that's a bank robbery." This came from Vin, who also doubled as my bookkeeper.

"That's fine—you can stay home. I'm going to look for a new life jacket, and while I'm there, I might have to buy a kayak to go with it."

"Good. While you're there, you can buy an SUV to put your new roof racks on," Vin said dryly.

"Thank you, oh wise money guru. I shall heed your advice and get one with a sunroof so we can admire the gear while we head south for the race." All of this banter was said with the freedom and excitement of going on a trip with new gear and cash in my pocket.

I wasn't manifesting wealth through my power of positive thought; I was a conscientious, hard worker. I enjoyed spending my money, and I assumed the inflow would never end. I was exceptional at training people and setting up corporate programs. I spoke at numerous company events and annual meetings. I worked long hours that afforded me the luxuries of having more than enough. I knew if I continued to work hard, money would always be there for me.

Until it wasn't.

My money surplus ended in the fiery disaster that toppled the World Trade Center towers. The budgetary line item "training and development" disappeared from many large corporations or was replaced with pressing needs for upgraded security and safety. My lucrative contracts were lost in an instant, along with other people's lives and businesses.

The post 9/11 period gave me my first experience of existing in an unstable, fluctuating economy that I could never have envisioned. This financial blow came at a time when I was loaded with cash liabilities. I had contract employees to pay, a leased truck, a monthly mortgage, and business expenses. I was caught with my pants down and was shocked at how fast things could change. I sold my house, turned in my truck, and scaled back my employees. Thankfully, I didn't have a family to support. I was able to manage by drastically changing my lifestyle, and I started on a path to find a new way to make money. It was a hard-learned lesson, and one I felt I wouldn't have to learn again. I would rebuild with caution and savings. I would be ready for the next round.

But I wasn't.

The next round didn't look like a world economic collapse, and it didn't happen without at least some advance knowledge, yet I was still completely overwhelmed by how quickly my life was turned around. The second time I incurred a loss of both my income and my job was when we chose to have a family.

No one told me that kids eat money and that my earning power would decrease by 100 percent. When I voiced my surprise, sane people said, "What did you expect? That you could have kids and keep working at the same productivity level?" Yes, I did! In my mind, I was a superwoman. I had always been able to generate income. I didn't think it would be difficult to manage a business, kids, and a marriage. Call me naïve or delusional, but I figured I would still be able to make a lot of money *and* have babies. I never anticipated that this whole kid thing would come with such a long contract.

Eight years and three kids later, REI might as well have been the North Pole. It would have taken a mythical fat man in a flying chariot to get me there to buy something. Day care, car seats, diapers, clothing, gymnastic classes, babysitters, and general kid expenses were eating away my wealth slice. I couldn't even say there *was* a wealth slice; there was an empty pie plate with an IOU in the bottom. I didn't need a budget; I needed a money tree.

Reverse Gift Cards

During those years I discovered the litmus test for how we were coping financially.

"Heather?"

"Yes, my love—what bidding can I do for you?" Sometimes I pretended my husband was royalty and I was his lady-in-waiting.

"Stop that. Did you pick up the mail?"

We lived in Cookie-cutterville, replete with nine different model home choices, small backyards, and a wall of super mailboxes that forced me to get out of my pajamas to pick up the endless flyers and bills delivered to our mail cube.

"No, but I will."

I didn't like getting the mail because there's never anything fun inside the box. It's usually just bills and an assortment fit-or-fat coupons, shiny cardboard advertisements promising me weight-loss results or a coupon for three extra-large pizzas with six-pack of soda.

I opened mailbox 5A and grabbed the monstrosity of envelopes that had been building up for the last three weeks. I tossed them in my bag and strolled back to the house.

When I arrived home, I started leafing through the envelopes. One stopped me cold. "AH! Shit! Shit, shit, crap. Dammit."

"What? Are you okay?" The string of profanity had my husband thinking I had hurt myself.

"Oh, no..."

"What? What is it?"

"Oh, this sucks."

"Would you stop it and tell me?!"

"Look."

I held up the square envelope. It was creamy and thick. The decorative writing looked like an epitaph on a headstone from the 1800s.

"Shit." Even my husband knew what it was. "A wedding invitation," he moaned.

My husband has a thousand more friends than I do. He's seen enough of these mail bombs to instantly recognize the signs that this was not a barbecue party.

"Crap. Who's it for?" He asked without actually wanting an answer.

I hesitated to check, because once I did, it would be like I'd signed for a registered letter. It meant we would be on the hook for, at minimum, an RSVP and a present.

"Your cousin. Why do you have so many cousins who like you? My family has three people, and you have three hundred."

My husband agrees with my wedding sentiments. We could go bankrupt with the number of invites we receive. He said, "Getting a wedding invitation is like getting a reverse gift card."

I sighed audibly.

Nothing is a better indicator of your financial status than the wedding invitation. When I had money, I didn't dread getting one in the mail, because it could be a fun outing with food and dancing. When my husband used to get invitations before we were married, he would shout, "Yeah! Open bar and tipsy ladies!" But now when I see that fat, square, linen envelope, I see dollar signs. I see a two-hundred-dollar wedding gift. I see an outfit that isn't denim. I see a babysitter and a hotel room. I feel pressure, not pleasure. Worse, when I see a wedding invitation, I know we are only months away from a square envelope in pink or blue for a much anticipated baby shower.

All of this would feel so much different if my current wealth slice had a little more pie on the plate. The wealth slice feels entirely manageable when there is enough. I long for the time when I don't have to sweat receiving wedding invites, paying the mortgage, or buying groceries.

Rich Mom, Poor Mom

"Heather, I want you to come and look at this area rug. I need to get one for the great room, and I just want your opinion."

"Sure, Mom."

I whispered under my breath, "Just let me get my Xanax."

The National Reserve would consider my mom a professional economy booster, but shopping with her is like viewing a streaming MRI on the workings of rational and irrational thought. A constant running commentary and corresponding nonverbal signals occur at every step of the purchasing process. She observes, assesses, obsesses, checks, and compares current and past sales. When she is done analyzing everything, she purchases.

I can't complain. Many times this shopping ritual has resulted in a lovely gift for my house or me. My mom has always been generous with her time and her money. From the time I was a little girl, she worked hard, didn't overspend, and made sound financial decisions. I've wondered whether her shopping skills are part of her wealth secret. If I had to guess, I'd say she belongs to an undercover society of master shoppers, a modern-day equivalent of the historical Knights Templar, like the Mall Maidens or the High Priestesses of Acquisitions.

As I watched her scurry around the decor section, I realized that my theory had to be true. She belongs to a world order of women with wealth. After years of observing my mom and other women of means, I believe there is a key to entering this secret society, and although it sounds strange, it appears to be the seemingly benign tea towel. Yes, a tea towel, also known as a cloth or in some locations a dishrag. It hangs in every kitchen around the world, on the oven handle or the utensil drawer pull, and is used for practically everything.

I know I'm not the only one who gets tea towels from her mother. For any reason or season, I have a fresh package of these stove curtains unceremoniously dropped on my kitchen counter. It's like my mother is leaving an offering to show the highest priestess that she will convert me into a woman of wealth. I wonder whether this "shroud of towel" is a code. Did Da Vinci leave a symbolic depiction of a wealth formula in the artwork on tea towels? Maybe I'm supposed to recognize a pattern and become a Priestess of the realm. Maybe this is the secret path to wealth.

"Here. These are for you. They have ghosts on them—for Halloween. The girls will like them, and you should really put away the ones with the Christmas holly now."

I thought to myself, *Really? The girls will like the tea towels? They don't even know how dishes get clean. A tea towel is a just another head scarf to them. Is this the code? Are tea towels a woman's secret handshake given to matrons of wealth? I don't have money, but my mother does. What the hell am I doing wrong?*

I've come to accept this weird exchange. Now every time I reach for a tea towel, I think of my mom and wonder if I'm missing what she's trying to tell me.

I was shaken out of my tea towel hypothesis and back to the task of shopping with my mom in big box hell.

"Heather, look—at—this!"

I would have, if I could have found her. At just over five feet tall, my mom is shorter than the shelves, and she often gets lost in tchotchke land.

"Where are you, Mom?"

"Right here! Now look at this wood elephant. I really like it."

"Uh-huh, that's nice. Let's look at the rug."

As I walked through the aisles of stuff, I saw a couple of lovely paintings, a rustic armoire with some nice, modern touches, and a kitchen table set that looked like it was out of *Mennonites Today*. I looked at everything. I ran my hand across the surfaces of the wood furniture, the sparkly crystal vase, the mosaic-style mirror. I touched it all. I thought about where I would put these niceties, and I longed to have a few of them in my home.

"What do you think about this rug? Oh, no. Look! Someone has put a hold on this. But I've been looking at it for a couple of weeks. I wanted this rug. I wonder if there's another one."

Her disappointment was palpable. This was *her* rug. It was the right length and color, the right thickness, and now she was clearly facing a sizable retail loss.

As my mother debated her rug options, I thought about the things I saw at the store that I wanted to own. I felt an incredible desire to just buy them. I wanted to put them on a credit card, bring them home, and see how nice they looked in my house. Then I would invite the neighbors over for a drink to show them my new purchases and let them *ooh* and *aah* over how perfect they were for the space.

But when I stopped and saw the things for what they really were, I became annoyed. I was annoyed that my desire for stuff was more about looking like we had money than actually needing the items. Our kitchen table was perfectly fine; I didn't need a rustic armoire, because I already had rustic cars. It was my inability to buy the items that was bothering me. I was frustrated that my wealth slice was more like a little piece of piecrust that had a small dab of filling left on one edge. I'd like to believe that if I did have the money, I would still choose to live a simpler life, uncluttered and devoid of excessive tchotchkes and replacement furniture. But what I wanted was the choice, and without expendable income, these were more things that I couldn't choose to have.

I see everyone else buying, buying, buying, and I wonder, is it just me? Am I the only one who feels like we buy so much and we already have so much? I struggle to live within my means, but I am constantly surrounded by signals and marketing campaigns that scream, "BE MORE! HAVE MORE! BUY MORE!"

I would have been happier if I didn't go shopping, happier if I wasn't lured into the great sea of endless choices at the store. I was happier at home, wearing my mommy uniform and my no-one-will-see-me ponytail. Shopping just reminds me of what I don't have. There will never be a storefront with a banner that says, "Heather, you already have more than you need—a thousand times over. Don't get out of the car; just go home."

Maybe I should start with tea towels. Once I learn to buy a quality, absorbing tea towel at a rock-bottom price, I will be fiscally responsible enough to manage my urges at Pottery Barn.

I get it now. The tea towels *are* a symbol for a secret society of wealth. Historically, they were recognized as a sign of money. They were hand-woven and embroidered on very expensive linen. In the late 1800s, tea towels were used only for drying the finest china in the finest homes. My mother would have been told by her mother to revere the tea towel, because it was an item of prestige and a sign of wealth. With this folklore embedded in her mind, she would have been tickled to find the historically upper-crust, tea towel now available in packages of five for a few dollars. Her drawers are stuffed with them in a possible attempt to stockpile the wealth.

Dry the china, line the bread basket, wrap up the wine bottle, wipe off the counter, or simply dry the dishes— a tea towel's uses are many. The tea towel comes from a time gone by when people valued the routine of a tidy kitchen and a home-cooked meal with the family at the table. It's a symbol of a time when the only money you could spend was the money you actually had in your hand. The tea towel is a symbol of wealth because it represents money—money that was meant to be respected, not just used to buy disposable items that get discarded indiscriminately. Tea towels make me think of my mom and Christmases and get-togethers in the kitchen, baking cookies, and feeding little hungry souls. Tea towels are the fabric I use to lift my fresh-out-of-the-oven, homemade, symbolic slice of wealth.

It would be a disservice to say that money can't but you happiness when the most current research shows that an upper-middle-class income makes you happy enough. Happy enough that adding to your money piles doesn't make you significantly happier.[19] Research on money and happiness has found that it's not absolute wealth that's linked with happiness, but relative wealth or status.[20] It's not how much money you have, it's how much you have relative to your neighbors. Money gives us choices, and choices can change our lives. Psychologist and author Barry Schwartz says it best: "Our culture of abundance robs us of satisfaction." Essentially, the more choices we have, the less satisfied we are, because we are always on the lookout for something better. I believe this paradox also keeps us from enjoying our own slice of wealth.

It is our culture's overabundance of choice that requires me to include more than money when defining my wealth slice. The only time I can find my slice of happy is when I remember to have perspective. Spending time with friends and family around the kitchen table, traveling to experience a different way of life, and taking the time to listen when people talk have all led me to greater wealth in my life, because each experience was about more than just money. Here is my advice on wealth: Stop going to the neighbors' homes. In fact, stop watching TV, stop going to the mall, and stop buying stuff. Un-American? Yes. Happier? Yes.

I believe the wealth slice must include your life challenges and triumphs. It's more than just your money; it is the legacy, the stories you tell, that you will leave to your family and friends. Wealth in North America is defined as what you own, but true wealth is slice of pie that combines not just your money, but your wisdom, experience, and vision, all built on a solid piecrust of perspective.

Unless I win the lottery or inherit a lot of money, my wealth slice will have to be acquired over time. I know I won't wake up one morning wealthy, but I will grow and build and even squirrel away a bit of money, until one day I will be doing okay. Not mega-rich, not living-out-of-a-shopping-cart poor, but okay enough to remember that being comfortable is a nice place to be.

My mom, Gail Korol 2011. This is my favorite picture of her.

CHAPTER THIRTEEN

* * *

Community: Charities and Other Things I Hate

When I think of the word "community," I think about people coming together for the greater good. I think about personal sacrifice for the benefit of the whole. Whether close to home or thousands of miles away, the options to help are limitless. But with so many pressing needs, where does one person start? Heal the sick? Save the planet? Educate people? With each cause, charity or community striving to make life better, it's become increasingly difficult to know where to begin.

The question, "Where do I begin?" becomes a circular argument. Protecting the environment seems paramount to our survival, as science is showing us that we are cooking the planet. Without a planet or hospitable atmosphere, the rest of the problems are moot but if the desire for environmental change requires expanding education, then world literacy must also be part of the formula. Of course food, clothing, and clean water precede literacy, because meeting basic needs is the bottom of the foundation and this puts us back at the beginning, where do you start when the solutions seems so complex? When one area appears to need immediate attention but requires a global framework to affect change, it feels too big to fix. Without global understanding, education, and tolerance, it feels like the scales are tipped against getting results that matter.

I'm terrible at my community slice. Not because I don't care, but because I feel like my one voice, my helping hand, doesn't make a difference to the collective. I feel overwhelmed by the magnitude of the world's problems and the energy required to make a difference. I often feel disgusted by the unjust struggles I read about around the globe, and I feel incapable of creating change.

I would love to eradicate cancer, feed starving children, save the tuna, and protect the rainforest, but sometimes giving to a charity feels like I'm putting money in a bottle, throwing it in the ocean, and hoping it will arrive at a *tsunami.*

Consumer advocate Erin Brockovich showed us that one person *can* make a difference, but it's a lot of damn work. Affecting broad social or environmental change requires a passion and dedication I haven't yet uncovered in my life. There are days when doing my part to preserve the earth or heal the world feels like trying to eat soup with a fork. The solution seems logical (get a spoon), but the process seems incomprehensible: apply for charitable spoon grant, rally a spoon following, define the parameters of the spoon, solicit spoon donations, have a spoon raffle, run a spoon event, envision the fork as a spoon, sell that vision, procure an environmental survey to ensure the spoon isn't going to negatively affect the fork, start the process, and document the change. Rejoice. The fork is now a spoon, and because of this change, the soup has become nourishment to a soul in need, instead of a bad utensil choice.

Building community should feel like a good thing; whether it's tackling a technical problem, an environmental concern, or an attempt to elevate the human condition, it should feel like the right thing to do. I need to find a way to make this vision a reality for me.

Recycle, Reuse, Re-Kill-Me

One of my greatest loves is the environment. If given the opportunity, I would squirrel myself away in a remote cabin and live like a pioneer—protecting, reusing, and recycling for the sake of the earth. Every time I envision my humble abode, I can't help wondering how I will equip it with high-speed Internet, bug spray, and Gore-Tex outerwear to keep the elements at bay. I'm a pioneer in spirit and a bug-hating, pillow-top-mattress-loving woman in reality. Like most people, I struggle with this duality: the need to be at one with nature and the simultaneous desire for the comforts of our generation.

A few years ago I was having a coffee with an adventure racing friend. As I sipped from my mug, I watched as Alex scanned the newspaper laying on the table.

"Alex, why are you shaking your head?" I noticed he was looking at a particular article in the life section.

He looked up and scowled at me. "Do you know why people don't like David Suzuki?"

Wow, this was out of left field. David Suzuki is the environmental Al Gore of Canada, except that he's never lost a presidential election due to hanging chads.

"Really, people don't like David Suzuki? I met him; he seemed nice." During the Ben Johnson steroid scandal, I was featured on *The Nature of Things*, a television show hosted by Dr. Suzuki. I was interviewed as one of the drug-free track and field athletes at the time.

Alex was not impressed with my fifteen minutes of fame. "He starts every one of his TV episodes exploring nature and flowers and little furry animal babies. You watch and you get drawn into the beauty of the story. Then once you're sucked in, he shows everything dying and decaying, all at the hands of mankind. When the show is over, you're depressed."

"Okay, but it doesn't make me not like *him.*"

"Yes it does, because he is the voice of the environment. He is the talking head that is supposed to inspire us to make the world better, but he's depressing as hell. His nature show fills you with awe about the power of our universe, then slams your heart shut by showing in detail how we are destroying it. People need a reason to get involved, not a program that makes them feel like there's no hope. People want the world to survive, most people want to help the environment but sometimes it's so hard. I can't tell you many times people have told me they hate recycling and do you know why?"

Now I was listening, because he had hit a sore spot. I still wasn't sure why I should dislike David Suzuki, but talking about recycling was a Whack-A-Mole winner with me. The day my city added composting to the weekly garbage separation program was the day I lost my mind about recycling. Not because composting was a bad idea—I wholeheartedly believe in creating less waste and recycling—but because now they were asking me to do one more thing in my seemingly endless day of to-do items. Managing our garbage already involved separating cardboard from plastic and glass, and now, in addition to breaking down boxes and rinsing cans, I had to take the gross garbage, the leftover scraps, and put them in a bin under my sink in a compostable bag. This compostable bag is a special bag that I had to buy in order to store rotten, stinky garbage in my house for a week until garbage pickup. One neighbor I talked to said, "Screw it. I'm not doing all that." Why didn't I just say "screw it" and dump the leftovers in the regular garbage? Because they also added a new rule that you could put out only one bag of garbage per week—one bag for the five of us. This one bag was to include every bit of mass-produced waste in our house, and all the rest had to be sorted for recycling or composting.

All of this plowed through my head before I answered Alex's question. "I could give you a hundred reasons why I love the environment but hate recycling, but what's your take?"

"Because environmental campaigns and initiatives sell you less of a future."

"Go on, please." I already felt like my Herculean recycling effort had eroded my give-a-shit quota, but I was listening.

"Think about it: when you recycle, it takes more of your time, gives you less satisfaction, and no one reduces your taxes. If you want to build an environmentally friendly house, it will cost you upwards of five times as much as a normal house. To do the responsible thing takes away from you as an individual but gives back to the world as a whole—in theory."

"Which is a nice premise, but why can't these initiatives bring more to me?"

"Exactly. Why isn't there a program that rewards you instead of punishes you for doing the right thing? Why is the right thing a sacrifice for the masses? Why is the right thing more work than the wrong thing?"

"Maybe it's always been that way. It's easier to take a shortcut than to go around the long way," I suggested.

We were at an impasse. I didn't hate David Suzuki, but I did wonder why it all had to be so complicated.

My husband and I would love to live off the grid, but we don't have half a million dollars to make it happen. Begrudgingly, I do what I am supposed to do with our garbage, and thankfully, we live in a place where people care enough to try to make a difference. I always question why our government doesn't use the giant burning orb in the sky as the greatest option of renewable energy. It's there for the taking. If we would just hurry up and run out of oil, we could get serious about harnessing the sun's energy in a way that wouldn't give us less. Other countries seem to have their eye on the sky—why aren't we keeping up?

Europe is twenty years ahead of North America in their recycling programs. In the early 1990s, Europe realized it had a problem. According to an article on the Emergo Group website, "Landfill capacity was shrinking, yet the amount of packaging and other waste generated by industry and consumers continued to grow." Faced with a pending crisis, Germany passed legislation to help curb the amount of packaging waste being generated. Essentially, the burden was placed on all European businesses to create less packaging when boxing, transporting, or displaying their products. This sounds great to me! This law works at all levels of business. You, as the consumer, can leave the packaging at the store where you bought the item. It then becomes the responsibility of the store to dispose of the packaging, which puts pressure on the producer of the product to create a less cumbersome package. There are fees and fines, but on the whole, more than 130,000 companies use this Green Dot program for packaging management.[21]

Hopefully leaders with vision can forge a path that will make a difference, helping to produce change in our waste management systems locally that will have a lasting effect globally would be a step in the right direction. The right initiatives could lead us to a place that allows us to have more but take less from our environment. Finding a way to coexist with nature without destroying it is a challenge with no easy answer. I will follow environmental initiatives that will reduce my output, but I also want to stop feeling abused by environmental standards that are thrust upon me but ignore the bigger problem of how they landed on my plate in the first place.

I'm Ebenezer Scrooge

"Andrea, when you're getting your groceries and they ask if you will donate a dollar to some charity, do you do it?" I was chatting on the phone with another mother who has two kids and runs her own business.

"Sometimes. Depends on if they catch me in moment of weakness."

"Exactly. I've just spent $257 at the grocery store, and then the sixteen-year-old cashier wants to know if I'd like to donate a dollar to children with cancer. I'm a middle-aged mom—do they think that because I'm hormonal and vulnerable, I'll say yes? My heart dies a little bit every time I read a story about kids with cancer but I feel angered when a mega-profitable corporation asks me for money. Why are they asking me for *my* dollar? Why don't they say, 'Once you spend over two hundred dollars, *we* will donate a dollar to kids with cancer'? Then I would say, great, I feel good about shopping at Grocery-Land."

Andrea jumped in with her view.

"I know. It's like they have you trapped with their finger poised over the 'add a dollar' button until you say yes or no."

"And then when you say no, you're an asshole for not saying yes. Somehow, you are choosing to let children die. Sometimes I say 'no thank you,' like they just offered me a cookie instead of asking for money." This conversation made me want a cookie.

I could hear Andrea putting the dishes in the dishwasher as we discussed our conflict over what constitutes charitable giving. "I bet rich people don't give a dollar. That's how they get rich," she laughed.

"Probably, but I wish it would stop." I paused for a breath, but my words continued to pour out. "Stop making me feel like I'm actually giving kids cancer. I'm not! Just because I distrust charities doesn't mean there isn't a need for them, but please, stop asking me for money on the phone, online, in the street, at the school, and at every checkout counter, including the grocery store!"

"Or Facebook. Ugh, friends asking you to support their bike ride across town to give money to kids that need bikes in Africa. It makes me insane. I want to say, 'Give them your own damn bike and leave me alone.'" Andrea's idea validated my assumption that I wasn't the only one who felt this way.

Giving to charities is a personal choice. I currently give to charities that I feel a connection with, but I want to be able to define my own obligations. I want to make a difference because it's the right thing to do, not because a charity has a broad-reaching marketing campaign. I'm not sure how it works at grocery stores, but with little effort they link themselves to a charitable cause and pass the 'add a dollar' on to me, the customer. The last time I checked, I was already giving them plenty of money.

I struggle with the negative feelings I have about charities. When I sense I'm on the extreme side of a debate, I wonder if I'm the one with the problem.

I asked my husband for his advice.

"Mark, what are you doing?"

"Just checking Twitter."

Mark and I are not obsessed with social media, but we do a fair bit of updating based on both personal and business interests.

"Why am I so uncharitable? I mean, I think I'm the most uncharitable person I know. Why do you think that is?"

This was a tricky question to ask my husband. First off, I had shaken him from Twitterland, which was like a never-ending comic book; second, I'd asked him to openly judge me. If he agreed with my statement, I would say he was not very supportive, but if he didn't agree with me, then I would say he was not telling the truth.

"Um, you did the walk for breast cancer with my mom. That was charitable."

"Yes, but that was your mom. She had breast cancer. I didn't walk because I believed that the money we raised would cure her—I walked because she wanted to do it, and dammit if I was going to let her walk sixty miles by herself. She may be tough as nails, but no one should walk that path alone."

"I guess, but you did it."

"I know, and thanks for trying, but I didn't do it to be charitable. I did it because she is family and I love her. This is what families do. They help. I loathed every second of begging and asking and scraping together the twenty-five-hundred-dollar minimum donation amount."

"I don't know, honey. Maybe you will get more charitable as you get older."

"Maybe. But how old?"

There is a recent charitable phenomenon that links every running, walking, and biking event with a charity. When a friend sends me a social network invitation and it starts with "Hey, everyone!" my finger moves unconsciously to the delete key. If I am receiving an invitation addressed *everyone*, I know what the next line will be. "I am running the (non-charitable company name here) half marathon, and I want to raise money for (giant, money-consuming charity name here)." Then the online invite will have links to various dollar amounts I can choose. There seems to be an unlimited number of these events.

I'm pretty sure people are hitting a donation wall. "David Hessekiel, president of the Run Walk Ride Fundraising Council in Rye, New York, estimates that in 2011 there were about fifty thousand '-athons'."[22] Only a small percentage of those who participate in such events do so because they want to raise awareness or money for the cause. Most people participate because the event is a personal goal. Raising money for the charity just happens to be a nice addition. If you do have the disease or disability that the charity is combatting, then you have my heartfelt sympathies, but it would be a stretch to believe that twenty-two thousand marathon runners are all there to support the quest to cure the problem.

Before you tear a strip off me and say that your spouse, child, mother, brother, or lover *does* have cancer XYZ, I say, "Me too." There *is* cancer in my family, there *is* diabetes and multiple sclerosis in my family, and there are lots of charities that my family could support from a place of personal connection. But I'm convinced we are going to run the well dry by asking everyone we know to give us money for an event with 'athon' attached.

A donation can be tangible but not actually charitable. Being charitable implies giving without expecting anything in return, be it a pat on the back or a plaque depicting the level of donation. To me, charity is about doing the right thing, helping someone that needs help, helping the environment because it's ours to protect, charity comes from a place in your soul that screams, "WE ARE ALL IN THIS TOGETHER!" Making a donation under pressure gives me the feeling that I *should* be doing this, that it seems like the *right* thing to do, but my soul doesn't scream anything, it doesn't even talk loudly – it just kind of shrugs and hopes the next time will feel more like it matters and less like I just watched Mariah Carey sing in a telethon.

The community slice is a tricky one for me, because I love to help people directly. I love to help in ways that make use of my talents. But I feel that if I cleave off one more bit of me to give to someone else, it will be the straw that breaks my hunched-over, Scrooge-like back.

While my family is still very young and demanding, the charitable part of the community slice is on hold. I still donate when I believe I can make a difference, I still offer help to friends in need, and I will continue to work on developing my charitable muscle. I know that when I'm in a calmer place, with greater expendable income, I will write a big, Oprah style check to the charity of my choice. But right now, my dollar is still my dollar. So please, in the name of charity, let me give it without being asked.

Check, Please

I'm trying. I'm trying to be more charitable, more environmentally friendly, and more connected to my community. I'm trying to think of ways I can make a difference in this slice. I wonder: If I started donating more often, would I feel good about my contributions, and would the upward momentum then take me to a new perspective? In an effort to test this theory, I started at my kid's school.

Each day the kids and I talk about the charitable events that happen at school and their importance, but I'm not sure the message is getting through to them properly. It has become clear that my girls aren't really sure why we raise money for things. They think that if you want something, you ask people for donations so you can get it. Recently, my girls wanted to get a cat, and I said they didn't have enough money to take care of a cat. They told me they would just ask people for money to help them out. They connected their own dots—if you don't have money for something, you just start asking for donations. With so many charitable events at their school, it's no wonder this has become a confusing topic for them.

One year I thought I had found a way to avoid the endless rounds of fundraising and still fulfill my resolve to be a more charitable person.

As I walked into the office of my girls' elementary school, I directed my positive energy vibe at the front desk receptionist. It was the first week of school, and I was determined to not only be more charitable but also more organized.

"What can I do for you?" The secretary was lovely. She knew the girls, and she always welcomed me kindly.

"Hi Debra. I was wondering if there's some way I could just write a check at the beginning of the year for all the fundraising events that will happen from now until June."

"I'm not sure what you mean."

"You know how there's about a hundred different events that the kids are supposed to raise money for, and then we're supposed to send in each donation separately with all the paperwork for each child?"

"I don't think there are a hundred, but yes, you mean raising money for our school programs and the various charities our board selects?" She backed away from the desk a bit. The other secretaries looked up, sensing a shift in the tone of our conversation.

"Right, of course. Is there a way I could just write a check for the whole year? You know, a check that covers everything for each kid?"

Debra wrinkled her face like there was a foul smell the air. "Well, no. I mean, each charity has its own collection process, and we can't divide up the money. No, you can't just give us a check."

"Right, okay. No check. I'll just wait until the papers and forms and pledge sheets come home and then send them in, right?" I acted like I was confused about how the whole process worked. Like this whole chat was a big misunderstanding, and my kids hadn't been attending the school for the last three years.

"Yes, that's right. Just fill them out as you get them, and return them on the appropriate date." She softened a bit, no doubt assuming that I was probably overtired or delusional to think that writing one check would be preferable to participating in the fundraisers.

"Great! Thanks for your help on this. See you tomorrow!" I smiled like a chipper mommy who cared about pledge sheets.

I left in disbelief. I couldn't write a check? It would have been so simple. Debra could have just told me how much, and I would have donated that amount and been done. I could have filled my community pie slice and never mishandled or forgotten about another purple photocopied form for raising money again.

When I arrived home, I called Tina. "Hi. I tried. I tried to give them money, and they wouldn't take it. They were actually offended that I wanted to just write a check for the year. Like I was going to miss out on all the fun of doing the events."

"Oh, lord, and now they think you're a lazy, lots-of-money mommy."

"I know. Funny. I don't even have any money, but I would give away my last dollar not to be *asked* to give away my last dollar."

"You're going to have to figure out why you are so uncharitable," Tina said, as I held the phone to my ear and lugged the recycle bin to the curb.

"I know. I'm trying."

Giving back is part of our genetic makeup; most people come preprogrammed to want to help. In times of crisis, whole communities rally to rebuild their community that may have been destroyed by Mother Nature, political discontent or acts of terrorism. People in a community donate time, money, and their emotional support when they can see how their efforts directly affect the outcome. There are great personal reasons to get involved, and there are legitimate causes that need our support, but I think bringing charity to a level that is tangible would be a big step in restoring people's faith in supporting their community and the desire to give.

Community: a slice of pie on the wheel of life. Giving back, helping, donating, recycling—these are things that should come from within. For me, this is going to be my "later" slice. When I am ready to nourish this slice, I hope to give back some of the knowledge, wealth, and understanding I have gained in my own life to a group or cause in need. I know it's in me. I've seen a glimmer of hope. My charitable slice is like a baby seed that needs a pot, soil, and some sunshine to coax it to blossom. One day that seed will produce a fruit, and the fruit will be used to make a pie filling that will be baked into my community slice. There's quite a list of things that have to happen before my seed becomes a slice, but I hope one day it will spring up, and I will write a chapter filled with charitable giving, bake sales, and kitty-cat rescues. I will find my worthwhile endeavor, and when I do, I will apply the passion I have found in my other slices. Stand back, world, I'm coming to help - just as soon as I plant my seed.

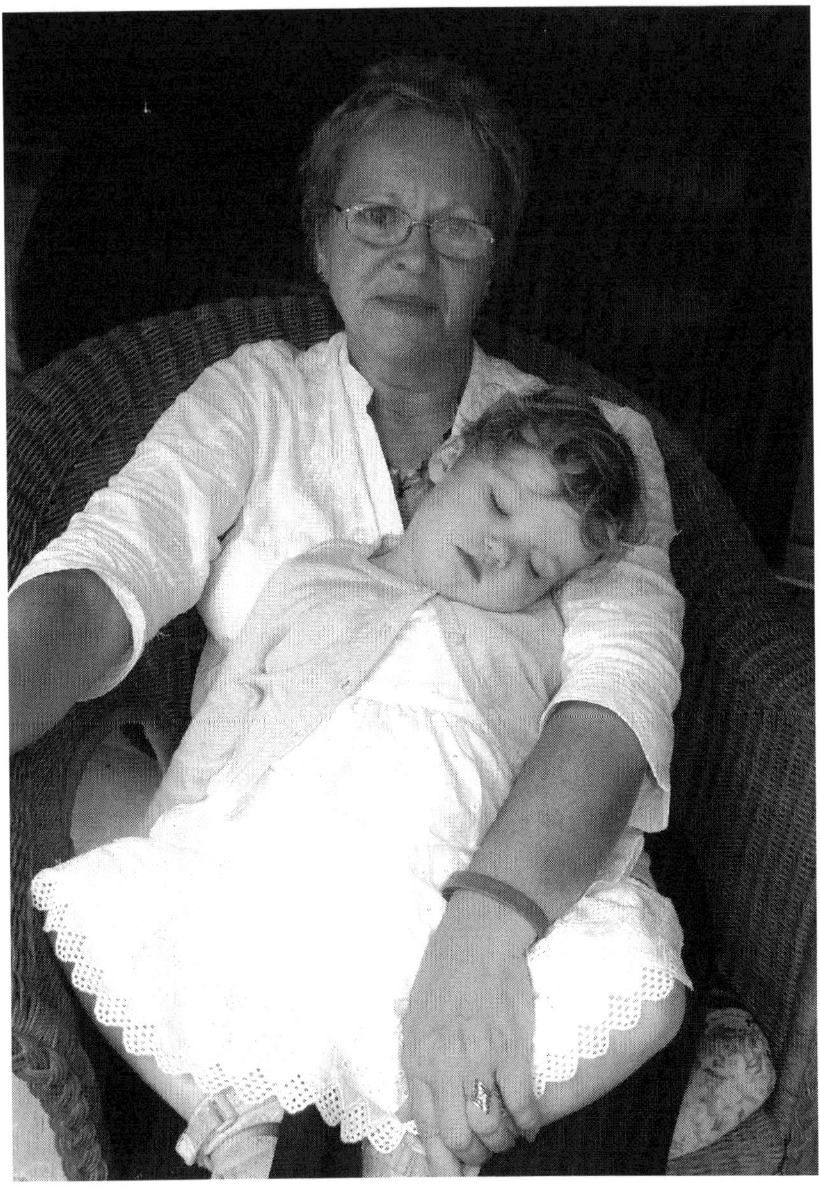

My mother in law, Donna Arnold taking a break with Ellie Arnold.
Original diagnosis of breast cancer in 2005, she is still cancer free today.

CHAPTER FOURTEEN

* * *

Leisure: Coffee for Breakfast, Wine for Dinner

Every day I try to carve out some time to do what I love. The things on this list are simple. They could include going for a bike ride, talking with my best friend, reading a book, exploring a new trail with the kids, having a coffee with my husband, or a glass of wine with friends.

In an attempt to capture more fun or passion in the leisure slice, I've considered the advice of self-help guides who ask the question, "What would you love to be doing right now if you had no other obligations?" I think a better question would be "Right now, what obligations are in the way of doing what you love?" The second question is tougher, because it's not asking what I would love to be doing if my circumstances were different; it's asking how I could change my circumstances so I could be doing what I love.

It's easy to think or talk about doing things you enjoy, but imagining and dreaming about your passions doesn't equal doing. To do the things you love, you have to make space for them; let go of the demands, the stuff, and even sometimes the people that take up the time and energy needed for you to breathe. Making space in your life means simplifying.

We all have our own list, but over the years I've come to acknowledge the activities that eat up time I could otherwise use for what I'm passionate about. These time eaters include (but are not limited to) birthday parties, cleaning the house (laundry needs its own book), dollar stores, and the biggie: worrying about what other people think.

I Have a Birthday Hate-On

Why would anyone dislike birthdays? Everyone is born, no one is not born. I assure you, Socrates or Plato would agree with this, but just because you were born doesn't make that day extra special. There are over seven billion people in the world and only 365 days in the year to share. If you divide seven billion by 365, it means over nineteen million people were born on the same date as you. That's like sharing your birthday with the entire state of Florida or more than half of Canada. And no, I am not a complete curmudgeon. I understand that when you are seven, your birthday is about the greatest thing in the world. But birthday expectations are out of proportion for a milestone in which the only requirement is being alive. Everyone should feel special in some way, but celebrating because you were born is not the same as celebrating a great triumph or a life-affirming accomplishment.

I find birthdays stressful. My own birthday is painful enough, but when I think about kids' birthday parties, I'd rather walk into a tank of hungry piranhas wearing Lady Gaga's meat dress than face what has become an insane ritual.

"Did Clara get an invitation to the birthday party for the twins?"

"No, I don't think so. Let me check." I dug around in Clara's backpack as I talked to Lynda, the mommy of Clara's best friend. "Shit. Yes, she did. Which twins are these?" There was an algae bloom of multiples in both of the girls' classes, and I never seemed to get them straight.

"Hannah and Lauren. The ones with the mommy who wears stilettos at pickup."

"Right. Are you going to take Chloe?" I asked Lynda.

"Yes, are you kidding? Three hours of me time? Of course I'm bringing her."

"I don't want to go," I declared, even though it wasn't me who would actually be going. "Three hours of me time is a ruse. It's a bait and switch. Three hours of free time equals two presents, clean party clothes, brushed hair, wrapping paper, and a card that I have to either force my kids to write or pay a small ransom to buy. Add that to the stress of the drop-off and pickup and the fact that I can't look like I just got out of bed when I get there—it's too much."

"Really? It's not that bad. Just grab a gift and drop her off."

I couldn't agree with Lynda. I was possibly alone in my birthday dislike, but I found the whole process time-consuming and insincere. The worst part is the goody bag. At the end of each party, guests always receive a small bag of what I refer to as 'goody garbage.' These bags are full of dollar store crap that is essentially scraps of paper and sharp-edged pieces of plastic. The bag enters the house, and then a day later it ends up in the garbage. The kids tell me the birthday party was okay but the goody garbage was awesome.

I'm not ungrateful that another mom has gone to the effort to make a special day for her child. I'm resentful of how we got to this level in the first place. I'm not even sure that my kids like going to parties. Parties are loud, screaming events where only the party girl opens presents and all the other children watch. Drool and spittle form on the corners of their mouths while they dream about touching the new toys that aren't theirs. I've had a mom tell me that my daughter hid under the table for most of the party because it was "so crazy." I understood, because I'd hide under there too if I had to watch twenty, five-year-olds, all high on helium, bashing the guts out of a piñata.

I didn't mention these things to Lynda, because she would have thought I was crazy, or whatever it's called when you don't like birthdays. Instead I sighed, "Yeah, right. Okay, I'll see you at the drop-off." But before Lynda hung up, she pierced my head with a question that made my palms sweat.

"Heather, what are you going to do for Clara's birthday?"

"Oh, lord—nothing?" I truly didn't want to do anything, but we both knew I would have to do something. I debated the least stressful solution—giving her cash and a cake. Would my seven-year-old believe that this strategy would be better than my planning a theme, cleaning the house, and getting the games ready, all the while acting angry and stressed while I tried to jam the perfect party into an already packed week?

"Ha! You're silly. Kids' parties are fun. Don't you love the looks on their faces?"

"No, because I can get all those same looks from the tooth fairy, the Easter bunny, and Santa. I can only be thankful that no one has invented the Secret Birthday Fairy."

I heard Lynda's kids in the background, crying because one of them poked the other one. She quickly signed off. "Gotta go! See you Saturday!" That was the nail in the coffin; the twins' party was on Saturday.

I've taken steps to simplify the birthday process with my kids. For starters, no real parties until they are six. Before that age, it's family only. My kids also have to choose a party or presents. If you choose to have a small party, then you don't get presents from Mommy and Daddy. If you pick presents, you can ask for the one special, amazing thing that you want, but you don't get a party with your friends, just a cake with family. I don't do loot bags, and I hold parties in the early evening on a school night. I read about a party solution that suggested asking each guest to bring four dollars, donating two to a charity, and giving two dollars to the birthday girl. I like this option. We need a collective party agreement between moms so that we don't have to one-up each other with party ponies, drop-in princesses, and loot bags filled with goody garbage. Oh, and no more parties on Saturdays, agreed? I try to protect our family time by keeping the weekends open for family hikes, bikes, or seasonal adventures.

There's a limit to what I will do for my kids' happiness, because it comes at the price of my own. When I take away the exaggerated process of birthday parties, I make space to be with my girls in a way that will hopefully become a memory they will keep with them beyond the dollar store high.

Embracing the NO to Get to the YES

I try hard to control the martyr gene that overrides some of my decisions and has me choosing the responsible answer over the fun answer. The shift from being carefree to contained happened slowly. For me, it started with my first business but quickly accelerated when I got married and had kids. Suddenly I was asking myself, *When did finding time to enjoy nature, friends, or family become relegated to scheduling it in iCal?*

The research says we are the least happy at age forty-four. It makes sense that the leisure slice takes the biggest brunt of this unhappy burden. Most people in their college years never have to consciously find ways to add enjoyment to their pie. Leisure comes easily, because most of the other slices barely exist. In your twenties you go to the gym, work at your job, and then hang out with your friends; you socialize, party, plan trips, and see the leisure slice as a given. At that age, it seems ridiculous to read a self-help book to maximize enjoyment. But as the responsibilities pile up, it appears people need a gentle refresher on how to have fun.

My husband reminds me of this any chance he gets. Mark and I share a passion for riding our mountain bikes. We met at *Gears* the local bike store, where the co-owners, Ira and Kevin thought we would be a good match. As a result, we find that going to the bike shop still gives us a tingle of excitement.

"Honey, do you want to go for a bike ride?" Mark peered around the corner as I worked at my computer.

"Yes! Really? Let me get my stuff. Are you going to put the bikes on the car?"

"Already done." If there's a chance of a bike ride, Mark will ignore even the most pressing responsibilities like groceries, car repairs, or work. This responsibility-shirking is annoying when he goes riding without me. But this day, I would be going too! I happily grabbed my bike shorts, gloves, cycling shirt, water bottle, helmet, shoes, and a pepperette. Pepperettes are like gas station beef jerky—salty meat sticks that constitute first aid in hot weather.

One pepperette will ward off the strongest leg cramps on humid, jungle-hot days.

"Mark! Do you want a pepperette?" I yelled to him as he grabbed the bike pump from the garage.

"Yes! Bring a couple."

"Okay, I have the trail map and all the gear. Should we get a coffee on the way?" I was excited and a bit giddy, because a coffee and a bike ride are pretty close to the perfect date.

We got in the truck. Mark put his hand on my leg and smiled. He looked at me like he was saying, "This is every reason I love you." It felt nice. This was our bond. We enjoy doing a lot of things together, but riding our bikes and sharing a coffee are the pinnacle. This was a giant slice of uninhibited fun.

As we unloaded the bikes and the gear, I felt the little spiny butterfly in my stomach that told me we were in for an adventure. The trails were dry and fast, and this meant we would be tucking in and only feathering the brakes. As we hit the berms and the sweeping downs, I felt the warm air heat up my face. I looked at the trees and the valleys and focused on the moment. Every pedal stroke was calculated in my brain and transferred to my legs. Every turn was as smooth and fast as I could handle. Mark was in front of me, and I followed his track through twists and turns. We laughed and whooped out loud as a big drop-off took us both by surprise.

"Wow. That was an awesome, leave-your-crap-at-the-door ride!" I could barely contain my smile. It was ear to ear, and the dry dirt on my face cracked when I opened my mouth.

"I love you. That was great," Mark replied.

My grin said more than words could. We rode back to the car and loaded up. We drove home, thinking about the moments that made up the day and how everything else just washed away. All the lists, responsibilities, and social obligations dissolved into the background; it was just the two of us, together on our bikes.

Most people spend too much time doing things they hate and not enough time doing things they love. I am worse than my husband at pushing this slice into a Tupperware container at the back of the fridge. I wonder if it's because of the multiple tasks we take on as women. I have to remind myself that it's okay to say no to life's less fulfilling tasks and yes to the ones that make my heart soar. This is not being selfish; this is being real about how much time we are given on this earth to enjoy our journey. This is being truthful about what is important to me.

The leisure slice slips away as we get older, because we forget to let our hearts tell us what is fun and fantastic. We let our brains and our shame tell us that other people's needs are more important than our own. The leisure slice is a reminder that it's okay to say no.

The "NO" Miracle

There are so many moments that steal time and energy from people: answering phone calls from telemarketers, reorganizing the dishwasher to cram in as much as possible, deleting vast numbers of e-mails that invade your inbox repeatedly. The list comprises small daily actions that seem like nothing, but if you add them all together, you come to feel their oppressive weight.

These life wasters eat up the remaining emotional and physical energy you have in your day, I call them life vampires and whether they are emotional, work or relationship vampires they conspire to suck the joy out of your fun pie. Forget surviving the zombie apocalypse—give me a how-to book on cloaking myself from the endless supply of life-draining people and tasks.

Among the things that take up so much of our lives is stuff itself. Getting rid of stuff in an effort to create space or simplify your life can be a liberating step. It allows you to let in the things you are passionate about. In our house, we battle stuff invasions regularly.

"What is this?" My husband was pointing to a volcano-like pile of small mismatched toys in the living room. He looked at me as if I had just landed on this planet from a galaxy devoid of matter.

I glanced at him as my face scrunched up and the sarcasm spilled out. "Honey, are you asking me what these toys are, or are you showing me that our kids left their toys in a pile on the floor again?" The air drained out of my lungs. I felt my body slump and my mind fade from our conversation. It was always the same. *Man sees stuff. Man thinks stuff is choking him. Man angry about stuff. Man throws stuff out. Woman stands there while children cry. Woman thinks man is selfish. Woman decides man should not have clean clothes and should look at toilet shit-ring for eternity.*

"They shouldn't just leave their stuff here. This is not their playroom." He was angry that there was kid paraphernalia littered about the house. He was also trying to find something that he had misplaced. These two factors were precursors for a brewing storm I like to call *Whose Crap Is This?* It was usually followed by *I'm Going to Throw All of This Out!*

"I know, honey. They shouldn't leave their stuff here, and I shouldn't have all my things on the bathroom counter, and you shouldn't have seven pairs of shoes at the front door." My self-righteous rhetoric made him simmer. It's not that I didn't agree with my husband, it's that I was tired of the repeated debate about how best to rid ourselves of stuff. In our household, somehow I've become the keeper of everyone's stuff, the knower of where everything is, including passports, extra keys, Scotch tape, and of course, the charger for every iPhone, DS game, and iPad.

"I'm going to throw all of this out!" Mark fumed. "Clara! Ellie! Get in here, please. Whose stuff is this?"

This is the worst question you can ask your kids, because it's an invitation for them to compete for the grand title of I-Don't-Know Champion.

"That's Clara's stuff." Ellie was the first to point the finger.

"No, it's not. Those piglets are yours, and the Lego pieces are yours too. I don't even play with Lego. I'm not picking it up, because I watered the flowers." Clara was defiant, and I was confused.

"Huh? Clara, what does watering the flowers have to do with picking up your toys?" I asked because at their age, logic wasn't a stepwise progression; it was more like a leap down a rabbit hole.

"They are not my toys, and I watered the flowers so they wouldn't die, and that's a hard job and I help around here." Her logic jump was stunning. Clara believed that since she did something yesterday to help around the house, she was automatically excused from helping today. If the logical leap worked for my kids and for my husband, I decided that I would apply the same concept to myself.

"Fine. All of you can take your stuff and put it in your rooms. Including you!" I stared at my husband, shooting him with my poison eye darts. "Get it out of my sight. Mommy's marble is shifting, and I would recommend that you all make yourselves disappear. Now!"

This incident started as my husband's fight, but my primal defense mechanism had kicked in. I'd had enough. Enough of listening, cajoling, asking, prompting, hoping, and sometimes praying that my girls would grab the reins and act more like working farm kids and less like spoiled princesses.

The kids grabbed what they could and scattered. They knew the ship was going down, and they ran upstairs like rats escaping the Titanic.

"Heather, we have to make this better. Please, help me understand what is going to make this better." My husband was asking because he wanted us to make a change together. He sensed that I needed support in our battle against the stuff, and he didn't want to exacerbate the situation—he wanted to help.

My anger was simmering below the surface, and my words were loaded with pent up frustration. "I'll tell you what I need. I need a cleaning lady. Wait, I don't need a cleaning lady. *You all* need a cleaning lady!" And that was it. I walked toward the kitchen, leaving my husband standing in the uncollected pile of inert dollar store toys that had started this snowball rolling.

"We need a cleaning lady." Mark muttered the same words as he put on one of his seven pairs of shoes and headed out to Home Depot for some therapeutic touching of things like power drills and pneumatic tools.

Twice, a cleaning person has saved our marriage. The first time we had two small babies, and we were both working full time. There was enough money to rescue our marriage from an impending stuff-divorce by hiring Rick, who came twice a month, and like a good marriage counselor, he scrubbed the anger and resentment out of the argument about whose job it was to clean the toilets.

Rick left when we hit a tight spot in our budget, but within a few years we were back on track and I was pregnant with our third baby. This time we preempted the divorce papers and started the process quickly. We found a new Rick, and her name was Maria, a Portuguese woman who wore a cross and soft slippers. I'm pretty sure she said a prayer as she crossed the threshold of our house.

"Okay. Hi, Heather. Oh, your girls are so beau-ti-ful and you are expecting another *princepessa.* This is so great. Yes, you need me here. I can see this." She clapped her hands together and looked around like she could turn dirt into wine.

I loved Maria right away. She was warm, smelled fresh, and brought her own mop. She didn't hold any punches, and she knew I needed help. Managing the business, our children, and my third pregnancy was too much for me. Our house looked like it needed to go through a car wash.

"Okay, I'm not gonna tidy your house, but I'm gonna really clean it, you know?" Her Canadian-Portuguese accent flowed like she was singing the Mr. Clean commercial.

Of course I knew. I knew that this woman *knew how to clean houses.* She didn't grow up in a family that just picked up their stuff; she grew up in a place where vinegar and warm, soapy suds were like holy water. A clean house was like God's house to Maria.

Each time Maria took over the task of cleaning our house, it afforded me the time to organize and toss the stuff that continually accumulated. After months of having Maria come to our home, she said to me, "Heather, you make me very happy."

I smiled at her as I asked tentatively, "Why? How could I make you happy?" I was thinking she must have enjoyed our pleasant talks about our families when she arrived.

"I like to work for you because when I come to your house, I know I make a difference. I go into other people's houses and they have vacuumed before I come. I just don't know why I'm there. But when I come to your house, you always need me. There's always *so much to do.* I leave and it feels good. It feels clean."

God bless her, because even though she insulted my domestic capacity, her efforts made us both happy. Each time Maria left our house, it was like a miracle had occurred on the premises.

"Mark! Maria's coming today. Do you want to go for a bike ride?"

"Yes! I'll get the bike pump."

Maria gave us the option to choose our fun slice. We gave up something that brought us no enjoyment to have the time to do something we loved. Of course, this came with a price tag. I traded a dozen different things to ensure that Saint Maria arrived at our house twice a month. I highlighted my own hair, and my husband did all his haircuts at home with the clippers. We selectively put our kids in sports that didn't cost an incredible amount of money and didn't require equipment like face masks or horses. We managed our choices in a way that opened up space. We simplified, and we are happier for it.

The leisure slice is the give-back slice to yourself. When you spend time enjoying life, friends, or adventures, it puts energy and inspiration directly back into your soul. My husband and I ensure that we have fun together. If we didn't carve out time for this slice, then we would most likely be divorced. It's that simple. As a couple, we need quality time together, and as individuals, we each need to seek out a sliver alone. Friends, bike rides, playing with my kids, sharing a glass of wine with my mom or a slice of pie with my best friend—these moments and memories are what keep me plugging away from one task to the next with the understanding that having fun is the fastest way to feeling happy.

Friends for Now or Friends Forever

When I ask people during a seminar what they are passionate about, two of the most common answers are "hanging out with friends" and "spending time with my family." This makes sense because some of our greatest memories are those that we share with the people that give us the latitude to relax and be ourselves. When people talk about the leisure slice, the two most common themes are family and friends, the two of the most common words I hear are 'wine' and 'coffee.'

Our friends Rachel and Kevin are neighbors who have become like extensions of our lives. Our kids are the same age, and we spend an inordinate amount of time in each other's homes. We are like family, but different—family without the pressures.

"Hey, honey, Rachel and Kevin want to know if we want to go over for a barbecue and some drinks on the patio," Mark said as he held his hand over the phone.

"Of course we do. Let me get some ice."

When we arrived at their place, we didn't pause at the front door; we just let ourselves in. We had their garage code and knew their secret hide-a-key place.

Unlike us, they were always renovating something. Rachel had an intense desire for the color of each room to match the latest home décor magazine, and Kevin was handy with a circular saw, brad nailer, and things that involved grout and tile plugs. As a couple, this was their thing they did together. When they fought, this was their safe ground, their glue.

"Hey, guys! Come on in!" Mark headed off with Kevin to talk about the latest in barefoot running and beer.

Rachel waved her arm. "Heather, come upstairs. Let me show you our bathroom."

This was normal talk with Rachel. She was open and honest and wanted me to see inside the most private vestibule of a married couple—the master bathroom.

I walked into a veritable garden of porcelain tile, granite, and craftily recessed lighting. The shower door was a wall of glass that spanned the entire room, and the bench seat inside had geothermal heated tile. It was like sitting on a hot rock while you washed away the day's troubles.

"What do you think? I'm almost done with the final paint coat, and then I'm going to put the trim back on and fill it, sand, and repaint. After that it's pretty much finished. I'm not sure about these handles; I was looking for something a little more subtle, but we had these left over from the cottage renovation and I thought, why not?"

Of course it was spectacular. It was magazine-ready, and from demolition to design, each step had been completed by their own hands.

"Wow. This is awesome."

I meant it. All of their renovations were masterpieces. They had an exercise room in the basement, a wine cellar, a three-tiered deck, a hand-built gazebo, and countless tile and backsplash upgrades. After much *ooh*ing and *aah*ing, we made our way back to the kitchen.

"Heather, a drink?"

"Oh, if you insist. I'll have a glass of red."

We settled in at their island counter in our usual places. The routine was like a well-choreographed dance, and we all knew the steps. It felt smooth and comfortable. We'd shared countless school recitals, birthday parties, play dates, bike rides, trail runs, games nights, dinners, and drinks together.

"Heather, do you want some sausages with this new honey mustard dip?"

Everyone knows I don't turn down a sausage appetizer. "Of course, and pass me the toothpick stabbers, please."

As I reached over and grabbed a tasty morsel, my eye caught a magazine on the counter. It was a nutrition magazine, and the cover had a picture of a toned woman with what could only be a set of D-cup breast implants surrounded by the heading, "Natural versus organic, which is better?" I recalled seeing that magazine earlier at their house. I remembered it specifically, because when I saw it I laughed out loud, even though no one could hear me. I was certain the heading was talking about food, but someone should have consulted the page layout designer.

The first time I had seen that magazine cover, I was alone in Rachel and Kevin's house. They were away and had asked me to feed their cat, Kona.

"Kitty? Here, kitty. Where are you?" I was on cat duty, and I couldn't find the cat.

"Hey, cat—you'd better not be dead, because *dead cat* is not on my good neighbor checklist."

As I went through the rooms looking for Kona, I paused, wondering why such an odd feeling had come over me. There was an incredible sense that I was in a stranger's house, except I knew what was in every cupboard and could find pine nuts without even thinking.

"Meow."

"Oh, good—you're not dead."

As Kona pounced down from the cupboard to the counter top, the emptiness was tangible. I could feel the silence, if that was possible. The house was still. I wandered about the rooms checking on things, seeing the calendar on the fridge and a small to-do list on the counter. That was when I noticed the magazine cover and its ridiculous headline, and I laughed out loud. The sound of my voice echoed in the quiet house, and it made me want to lock up and scoot out immediately.

"Hey, cat, I have to split. It's creepy in here."

I couldn't help but think about how we find friends because they strike a chord in us that makes us feel grounded and safe. Friends keep us energized and engaged, and yet stable and calm. With no one in the house, it felt like nothing. It felt like a void in a place that was meant for laughing and music and kids screaming and coffee brewing. It felt like the life had been sucked out of the house.

The general banter at the kitchen counter continued, but I was stalled in my thought about the empty house.

"Mark, did you work last night? Any big fires?" Trevor asked.

"Yeah, we had a huge fire at a plant in the city. Four alarm."

The feeling I had on that day in the empty house made it clear to me that material things mean so little in a world filled with stuff. A home without friends is just a structure. Without the people that you care about, it's just a place to live. It solidified my true sense of what was important.

It was at this moment that I noticed Rachel was distractedly bruising mint, and mojitos weren't even on the drink list.

"Hey, Rachel, what's wrong? You seem distracted." I took a sip of my wine as she looked up from her mint.

"Nothing. Just, you know, getting things sorted in my mind."

"Why? Are you guys moving?"

"What? No, we're not moving."

"Yes, you are. You guys are moving. I can smell it."

"Why do you have to do that?"

"Do what?"

"Why do you have to be right?"

It turned out that they were moving to Boston in eight weeks. We knew that Kevin's job as the general manager at a company in Canada would lead to a move to groom him for a corporate climb in the USA, but we were heavy-hearted about the news. We started to feel the impending separation immediately. I wondered whether our friendship would survive the move. I mean, not only was there going to be a giant geographical divide, but now there would be new neighbors and new experiences.

It all happened quickly. There were drinks, dinners, goodbye parties, and goodbye tears. The kids didn't quite understand the full implications of the move, but soon they began to understand that their first true childhood friends wouldn't be living down the street anymore.

When Kevin and Rachel left for Boston, we decided the time was now or never to move to a town that could give us more of what we wanted out of life. We moved to a place that had more bike trails, ski hills, and beaches. We moved to a town that was smaller, less congested, and into a house that gave us a bit more space. They moved, we moved, and we both got new neighbors.

Moving is tough enough, but getting to know your new neighbors can be a gamble that may not pay off. You can never be sure whom you will be living beside when you plunk down in a new town.

I was outside with my girls when I spotted our neighbor out walking her dog. Her house is directly beside ours.

"Oh hi, my name is Heather. Nice to meet you. I see you out walking your dog sometimes. My girls love dogs—would it be okay if they pet her?"

"Sure! We have rabbits too. Oh, my name is Esther." She reached out her unleashed hand to shake mine.

"Nice to meet you. I see your husband outside sometimes but we've haven't met yet."

"That would be Ken. He loves the outdoors, Ken is a falconer."

Since I was born and raised in Concreteville, I thought maybe she was telling me her husband belonged to the local rugby team. "Mark would love that. He used to play rugby in university."

She looked at me, tilted her head with the confused look people give you when they aren't sure what you mean, and smiled. She didn't say much while the girls lavished hugs and strokes on Roxy the dog.

"Thanks for the doggie fix. I'll be sure to tell Mark to drop over when he's home," I said as we headed back to our house.

And that was it. Everything seemed pretty normal.

"Honey, I met the neighbors. They have four rabbits and a dog. You should talk to Ken, he belongs to the Falconers."

"He's a falconer? Really?"

"No—yes. I guess. Can you believe they have rabbits? Wait. Do you really think they have falcons?" I thought falconers were from the Dark Ages—or the Middle Ages, or whatever time existed before flushing toilets and light switches. People have falcons?

The next day the doorbell rang. It could only have been our new neighbor, because perched on his arm was a bird with talons that could carry away our baby.

"Hi, you must be Ken? I'll just get Mark. I'm pretty sure he would like to meet your, um, bird."

I raced to find my husband. "Mark! It's Ken, and he has his falcon, bird, thing. Hurry!" I sprinted around the house to find my phone in order to capture the moment of Mark meeting Ken and Ratchet.

Ratchet turned out to be a hawk, not a falcon, but Ken was still called a falconer. Ken was wearing what looked like a bulletproof glove with a massive bird clutching his arm. Ratchet had a leash on his foot, and Ken held the other end with his hand. I mostly stood there thinking, *Don't look it in the eye—right? Don't look giant birds in the eye. Or is that charging elk?*

My bird-of-prey education began as the boys unraveled the secret world of falconry and I listened. Mark was looking at the bird in awe. "Wow, this bird is awesome!"

"Yeah, thanks. He's pretty powerful. See his back claw here? This is the one he uses to spear his prey, and then he uses the front ones to close around it like a hand."

"So you send him off to eat, and then he just comes back?"

"Yes and no. You have to make sure he's hungry. I weigh him first, and if he's too heavy, I don't send him out to catch anything."

"Why?"

"Because a full hawk won't come back." Ken smiled, and Mark understood immediately, but my head was full of questions. *What does he catch? Pigeons? Cats? Mice? Babies?* I intruded on the man science for a moment. "Hey, Ken?"

"Yes?"

"What does Ratchet eat?"

"Well, when he's not catching something in the wild, I have a freezer full of quail."

"He eats frozen quail?"

"Yes, but it defrosts pretty quickly in this heat."

"Like a quailsicle?"

"Yeah, kind of." Ken smiled.

Mark apparently thought that was enough of my questions. He got the conversation back on track about understanding Ratchet's hunting capacity.

"Right, so you send him off to hunt?" Mark asked.

"Yes. When he catches something, I have to track him and take it away and then give it back to him. That's why he wears this bell on his foot."

Ratchet wears a bell that sounds like Christmas jingle bells. I quietly mumbled, "Ratchet bells, Ratchet bells, Ratchet all the way."

"If he didn't have the bell, I might never find him, because he cloaks his prey while he eats it."

My husband tried to cloak his own shit-eating grin while he listened to the most incredible man talk about falconry. I surmised that Ratchet's jingle bell would be like the ice cream truck for Mark. My husband would hear those bells and go running out the door crying, "The ice cream truck, the ice cream truck," but it would come out, "Ken is out, Ken is out, and he has quailsicles!"

"The bell helps me find him and also keeps me from stepping on him, because I would never see him if there was any undergrowth." Ken looked over at Mark. "Do you want to hold him?"

Ha! Does my husband, the man who drives a Land Rover Defender, hunts wild game, and drinks black coffee, want to hold a hawk?

"Okay, let me get this on camera." I said. "We wouldn't want to miss this Facebook moment."

I snapped some stills and then got the video rolling.

"This is awesome! Hello, Ratchet. Can I pet you?" Mark was giddy as he said to me, "Honey, who knew the new neighbors would have a hawk?"

That night I posted the video and still photos of Mark with the hawk gripping his forearm. He face was alight with the excited look of a ten-year-old. The words were out to the world: "Who knew the new neighbors would have a hawk?"

The next day I saw that the first person to post a comment was our old neighbor, Kevin. We had recently visited Kevin and Rachel in their new Boston home and had a fantastic time. We played horseshoes and bocce ball in their welcoming backyard, and hung out and jammed to the video game Rock Band while we sang the night away. We drank wine, and the boys tested an eighteen-year-old Scotch. The kids played endlessly. Our visit took place only a few months after they had left their old home, and I still wondered whether their new lifestyle could accommodate old friends. I had my answer when I saw Kevin's comment on the Facebook video.

"Yeah, but can he play Rock Band, drink Scotch, and ride a mountain bike?"

Fun, It's Good For You

If family is like blood, then friends are like oxygen. They can keep you alight when the days seem dark. They can raise your spirits or remind you that you are not alone. The leisure slice should be so easy to fulfill, because you could literally just eat pie. You could drink coffee, have a slice of pie with ice cream, and then wash it all down with a nice glass of wine. But people don't; they eat pie standing up while they scroll through their e-mails and unload the dishwasher. If we all worried a little less about what other people think, we could spend a lot more time enjoying what we personally find fulfilling. I know birthday parties make some people happy; I know that organizing houses makes others giddy. Social obligations and time eaters need to be defined in your life, and you need to make your own decision on what needs to go.

If you still find it hard to know what would make you happy, then there is no harm in trying different things. One of the greatest ways to experience the joy of life is to learn something new. Maybe you've always wanted to fly-fish, paint, or write—you can always try it out and see if it fits in your slice. Build something, sign up for a class, try a new recipe, go to a play, go for a hike, hang out with people who make you feel good—it probably won't take a lot to get excited about finding the fun in this slice.

The leisure slice is about more than just doing things; it's also about *not* doing things. It's more than having stuff to do; it's about getting rid of stuff and loving what you do. Friends, family, getting outside, and finding my own sense of calm are all things that fill my soul with unmitigated joy. I will make sure I grab this slice by its pinched crust, stuff it in my smiling face, and let the filling spill down my chin.

Mark with Ratchet, 2012.

CHAPTER FIFTEEN

* * *

Spiritualism: Death Sucks

You can hang out in an ashram, meditate in a sweat lodge, or Zen yourself with calm and serenity, but there is nothing more life-affirming that will drag you to the edge of spiritualism than death. We seek calm and a sense of connectedness through yoga, meditation, and religion, but we find *true* life meaning when we pause to reflect on the inevitable. It's the greatest reminder that the whole pie may seem meaningless unless you find your own spiritual slice of happiness.

My Greatest Fear

"Hey Dad, I love you."

"I love you too. Now go and win."

It might have been hot or cold, sunny or rainy, I couldn't really say, but the last day I saw my dad, I knew he was happy. The local newspaper had caught a picture of me mid-flight in the long jump, and there in the background of the photo was my dad, sitting up against the fence cheering for me. He was on a day pass from the hospital to watch the biggest day of my track life, and my mom had managed to get him on the field so he could see me fly. I brought the article with our photo to the hospital, and as he slapped the paper with joy, a smile spread across his face as tears came to his eyes. We had been captured together, father and daughter, forever in print. My dad was my biggest fan. He believed I couldn't fail, and even if I struggled and didn't win a race, he would make up a million excuses for my loss. In his mind, it was never acceptable that someone could have run faster or jumped farther. My dad thought I was the greatest.

His birth name was William Michael but his nickname was Silly-Billy. The collection of books on his shelf included studies in philosophy and English literature as well as comic books and joke magazines. He was an athletic man with dark hair and a lean body. He liked to dance to music wearing giant, old-school headphones while he dubbed a tape, but he was just as happy to people-watch at a crowded mall.

My mom and dad would throw house parties in the seventies when my brother and I were little kids. There would be disco and drinks, and my dad would hand out whistles to everyone so they could "toot-toot heeeey beep-beep" to Donna Summer. His idea of being funny was to ask one of my mom's friends if she wanted to see his stamp collection, and then he'd take her upstairs and have her lie down on the bed and look up at the ceiling, where he'd pasted a one-cent stamp. He was silly over serious, and he'd choose creative over stuffy any day.

He lived with juvenile diabetes from a young age, and he was one of the unlucky diabetics that seemed to suffer from early complications of the disease. He had his first major heart attack at the age of thirty-two, I was eight. That night my mom had the heartbreaking conversation with us and told us that our dad was probably not going to live. It seemed strange and confusing, and at eight years old, completely unacceptable.

My Dad made it through that night, and each month he got marginally better. As a family, we worked around his visits to the hospital and watched as his health faded and rallied. The physical and psychological effects of his illness were lost on my brother and me—we knew he was sick; we just didn't get what that meant. Our lives moved forward, and my dad was there as we grew out of the innocence of childhood and into the awkwardness of being teenagers.

One evening my dad I were watching TV, a movie about ghosts.

"Heather, what do you think happens when people die?"

"Nothing happens. You just die."

"Really—that's what you think? That people just die, they don't go anywhere?"

"Sure, they go into the earth and then worms eat them."

I was fifteen, and biology was my new religion. I couldn't imagine it any other way. Biology was logical, and at fifteen, overflowing with hormones and confusion, I thought science seemed like a solid answer.

"So you think we just die and then there is nothing, just darkness?"

"No, I think we die and then we decompose and then we are part of the soil—that's it. What more could happen? We become part of a tree?"

My snarky teenage voice made it evident that the discussion was over. I was right, and my dad was stupid.

Now, sitting here, I believe I can feel what he might have felt in that moment. The look on his face said everything, but at the time I couldn't understand. I'm sure he wanted to grab me, hold me, hug me, and tell me that I was his angel, his kitty cat, his best little girl. I was his gymnastics superstar, his math wizard daughter. My dad probably wanted to say a thousand things like, *You know I'm going to die soon. How can you be so sure nothing happens? Don't you want to believe that I will be in heaven and I will talk to you? I don't want to die. I don't want to lose my daughter, my son, my wife, my family, my life. I love you all so much, and I'm not going to be here. Why can't you see that? Why can't I tell you I love you so much and that soon I won't be able to tell you anymore?*

But he didn't say anything. In that awkward zone where a teenage daughter is outwardly so full of self-assurance but inwardly so fragile, maybe he knew that I couldn't handle it. We never talked about him dying. There was no Google search on how you approach these topics. In that era, lots of things were left unsaid because it was easier. Maybe it was better that way. To me, it didn't matter, because death was an abstract concept. I didn't want to hear that someone I loved was going to die.

If you are lucky enough to have your father present in your life, then you might have a bond or tangible memory that has helped shape who you will become. My dad captured a little girl's dream—he filled me with hugs and tickles and silly games and love. He gave me permission to think differently, to see the world and ask, *Why not?*

I was eighteen years old when he died. He was forty-two. I left for Arizona on a track and field scholarship on a day like any other in September, he died that same year in November. In my heart, I had known that he would probably die before I came home; not that anyone told me, but I could sense that he was on borrowed time. Before I left, I asked my mom if I should still go. She said, "You are his shining light. Of course you should go. He would want nothing less of his track star."

A few days before I left on my flight to Arizona, I showed him the newspaper article featuring both of us in the photograph. He was elated and proud. I had won three medals that day and qualified for the Pan-American junior games. Walking out of his hospital room was like entering a vacuum chamber. The air was sucked out of my lungs, and my heart seared with pain. How could I leave? How could I be the 'world's greatest daughter' and still go? How could I want something that seemed inconsequential compared to my dad? Why didn't I just wait? Why didn't I stay and be there and spend time with one of the most important people in my life? How could I be so selfish?

While the pain of my decision to leave was real, I still chose to go. At eighteen years old, I was teenager-invincible. No one needed anything from me, and more accurately, I didn't have much to offer. It was such an innocent, selfish time, except for this little reminder in the back of my head: my dad was sick, and he wouldn't be around forever.

I packaged away the bad thoughts of what could happen, and I did what mattered to me. I trained every day for track. I reviewed video footage of the best sprinters so I could visualize the way they ran, how they moved, and how they won. I ate toast with peanut butter every day after school because one of my Olympic role models said that was what she ate. I skipped normal high school socializing and dreamed of qualifying for the Olympics, because I was that good.

When it came time to make a decision, I knew the easy answer would be to stay, but I wanted that scholarship. I knew my dad would want me to do this. Maybe I left so I wouldn't be there for his passing. Maybe I knew if I stayed, I would never leave afterward. I can't say what would have happened, because I wanted this chance to take on the world, to show everyone that I could be the best.

As I flew home for the funeral only two months after that day in the hospital, all I could think was, *I want my dad back. I want someone to think I am the greatest.* When I left for Arizona, I believed I was all grown up. When I arrived back home, I curled up on my mom's lap, wrapped my arms around her, and cried like I was six. She hugged me and said, "Oh, my baby, Daddy loved you. You made him so happy."

Sobering Thought

Today I am almost the same age as my dad was when he died. This is a sobering thought. I am forty-one years old with three kids. I can't imagine dying now. If I died, what would happen to my life pie? My babies? My husband? My family? How would anyone know which baskets held the clean, unfolded laundry and which held the dirty? Who would schedule play dates, birthdays, doctor appointments, grocery shopping, and day care? Who would handle the seventeen pieces of paper a day that arrive in each kid's backpack? How would anyone ever find anything—Lego man's head, my husband's wallet, keys, or iPhone, the baby's double-sided soother? If I were dead, I wouldn't be there for little-kid hugs and hand scrapes, story time, or morning "Mommy, are you awake?" snuggles. I would miss my little stinker in her one-piece sleeper, fresh from her bath. How could they ever cope without me?

Death can be so overwhelming to imagine that days, even months, go by and I'm not touched by it. I tuck away the thoughts that bad things happen, and I assume that the status quo will never change. I get wrapped up in my routine, my job, my lists, and I gladly go about my days in a blur and a rush to get things done. Yet it happens, without fail: every day, people die. Neighbors we give a wave to but hardly know, the mother of twins in the day care group, the guy who works on the second floor in IT—they die. Selfishly, they die without warning, like a thunderclap that scares the crap out of you in mid-afternoon while you're reading a book. They interrupt your routine of ticking off the to-do list as they drop the death card squarely in your lap.

I hate this. Selfish? Of course, because if it wasn't for these pesky "dead people" reminders, I could pretend this won't happen to me. Their deaths are like a poke, a prod, a glancing blow on my sense of stability. One minute these people are here, essential to someone's day, and the next they are a whispered conversation at the water cooler. These deaths terrify me. It's like someone knocking on my head and yelling in my ear, "WAKE UP! THIS COULD BE YOU!"

When I hear of someone in my community who has died, it's like little electric shocks. It makes my spine tingle and gives me those unsettling butterflies in my stomach. I call them sideline deaths, or deaths on the periphery. They lead me to repeat hushed stories to others about how I *almost* knew this person and then "poof," they just died. I can hardly believe they are gone, because I hardly knew they were there. These losses are the ones that make me pull my family in tight, close ranks, and reflect on my own health and happiness. These seemingly random deaths allow me to lie in bed at night with my husband and talk about my own death without actually believing I might ever slump over at McDonald's.

We talk about things like my funeral wishes. Do I want to be cremated? Do I want an open casket, donations, pine box, flowers, music, an urn? Photo collages, video collages, snacks, alcohol, a post-funeral reception? Then we discuss more twisted things, like who would my husband marry if I was gone and maybe it would be a good idea if he found someone that liked to cook and clean and didn't write books. Helping my husband envision his future, not-dead wife is one of those conversations you hope never comes to fruition.

It's during these moments that I realize I am happy to have anything going right; I have perspective because I know there is something to be happy about. I'm not dead, nor is anyone in my immediate family. When death becomes part of your inner circle of friends or family, it's soul-crushing and paralyzing. For me, it's the paralyzing fear that people die and the world still goes on. That I am wasting my precious days worrying about finding the perfect hallway chandelier or wishing my neck had fewer chins.

Healing

After my dad's funeral and couple of weeks at home, I went back to university. It was hard. Hard like breathing wet cement, in a tunnel, underwater. Hard to move, hard to concentrate, and hard to understand that life seemed to go along without pause or thought to my pain. I poured my anger, my frustrations, and my loneliness into my running. I showed everyone what a person could do with this raw emotion when it was directed at a goal, and my goal was to win. People tried to comfort me, but I wasn't interested. How could they even begin to know what it was like to be me? It was inconceivable that anyone had suffered before me or had felt the kind of confusion I felt. For me, the idea of spiritualism or the platitude that, "God has a reason for everything" was a word Band-Aid that couldn't lift me, or bring me comfort. Death sucked.

At the time, I wasn't old enough or mature enough to understand that my dad was more than just a parent. Twenty years later, I can see that my dad was a lot of things to a lot of people, but when I was eighteen, this person was just my dad. He was the guy who thought the world was mine for the taking—a man who wanted everything for me that he wouldn't have. His death was an early awakening that stung and ached and smacked me in the head with a reminder that life could be really, really short.

Everyone talks about the five stages of grief, as described by psychiatrist Elisabeth Kübler-Ross. Forget the five stages—I needed fifty. Where in her theory was the "miserable pain and suffering" stage? Where was the "I can't shampoo my hair because lifting my arms seems like a Herculean effort" stage? What about the "I'm still grieving, but everyone else has forgotten and can't understand why I don't want to go out" stage? Or the "I'm trying not to cry while people make well-meaning toasts about *fill in dead person's name* at Christmas, birthdays, and other holiday nightmare" stage? I guess those were all conveniently included under the umbrella titled 'grief.' Grief felt like a very small word to encompass the heaviness and gravity of death.

George A. Bonanno, a professor of clinical psychology at Columbia University, argues that the stages of grief do not exist. Bonanno's research shows that most people who experience a loss do not grieve, but are resilient. He states that if there is no grief, there can be no stages of grief.[23] Huh. No grief, no stages; just resilience. How can this be true? The only way I could imagine not suffering pain from the loss of a loved one would be if everyone were suddenly struck by a virus that turned people into zombies and the world was exploding. World calamity would leave little time for grief. After reading Bonanno's research, others have stated that far from being misguided, the idea that humans are resilient is obvious.[24] Of course we are resilient; we continue to live and breathe and hope and cry. We want to feel whole and right and solid, but death shakes that out of us. It takes our equilibrium and turns it upside down and gives us the worst possible case of heartache, with a stabbing side of depression.

Where does that leave me? I have experienced death *and* shown resilience, but I've also crawled, scratched, cried, and wandered through the five stages. If you've never experienced the death of someone very close to you, then it might be hard to say how you would react. Losing a close loved one is like joining a really bad club: the Death Club. You can't relate until you join the club. It's similar to the Parenthood Club and the often overlooked Small Business Owner Club. The list could go on and on. Joining any of these clubs can be a time of great awareness and growth. But the Death Club is a formidable one, because it forces you to look at your pie and ask, *What slices are important to me right now?*

From my experience, losing a person who is intrinsically part of your life brings a new awareness of death and the affects it has on your perspective. It's hard to explain to someone what it feels like to lose a part of your soul but once it happens, you understand that finding some happiness, even one moment of happiness in your day, is paramount in moving forward. This is the only answer to finding a new normal. Without tiny baby steps toward healing (which to me is a hollow word for feeling less like dying yourself) you will be stuck in the pain, stuck in the cycle, not even inching forward to a new reality.

I often wonder whether we as a society would do better with death if we didn't perpetuate the idea that our loved ones were still with us by building shrines, keeping video and photo montages, and purposely revisiting images of the newly dead. Would we cope better using the natural resilience unearthed by Bonanno's research? Would we move through the theoretical stages of grief faster if we weren't constantly bombarding our senses with shockingly real monuments of our loved ones' living successes? Shrines, photos, and mementos can help us keep the memory of their spirit alive, but it can also keep us from making new memories. A surprising number of people save voice mail messages from loved ones in case it turns out to be the last thing they said to them. My mother saved my dad's voice on the answering machine tape—I think it is still in a keepsake box to this day.

When people die, we forget what they sounded like. We slowly forget the sharp images of what they looked like. As time moves on, we forget - even when we try so hard to remember. In my opinion, this gentle fading of their image is part of healing. Allowing ourselves to forget their look, their sound, their touch, and their smell, doesn't mean we have forgotten them but it gives us space to hold their spirit in our hearts.

Should we let our dead die and move on, or should we hold them strong and close to us through photos and old videos? Modern technology has created an unending capacity to keep our dead *in memoriam* forever. Facebook, for example, includes millions of ghost pages that belonged to users who have died. People die, but their pages don't. To those caught unaware, it would seem that they are still right there in cyberspace, just one comment away.

When I think about my dad, I remember moments. I lived in his presence for two decades, and yet only a handful of vivid, clear memories remain. I remember moments of laughing while watching TV, flashes of him staying to watch gymnastics class, and feelings of love—just snapshots of our time together. I recall one day when I was small, I asked for a hug and a kiss and he said, "Big hug only. Daddy just had a coffee, and he has stinky coffee breath."

I remember thinking, *Why would anyone want a drink that would make you stinky?*

What I wouldn't give now to share a coffee and a slice of pie with my dad.

When I'm moving through a new chapter in my life, I cry about the loss of my dad. I cry because I love life and I wish he were here to taste and experience this slice that I have created. I cry because today, as a mother and a wife, I know what it took for my mother to be resilient. Only now can I even begin to understand what it might have been like for her.

I cycled through the five stages of grief, and I used resilience to successfully get through the pain of returning to university after the funeral. Stages and resilience: each had its place. It's from my dad's death that I have been able to remember how important my slice of spiritualism is to my life path. My dad had a moment of genuine joy when he saw the photo of us together in the newspaper; this is a good reminder that finding inner peace, or God or Buddha or Allah, doesn't require rituals or manuals, but can be as simple as reflecting on one tiny moment of happiness.

Hiding from Death

There are those far above my status or faith who say they embrace death. They extol passing from this realm as a natural end or new beginning in the circle of life.

I'm not so good with death, and this is the part that I don't like to tell anyone: I'm so fragile when it comes to death and dying that when it's someone else's gnawing anguish, I'm selfishly happy it's not mine. I'm relieved I don't have to feel that hollow, angry pain.

When Tina called and told me her sister Laurie had suddenly died, I was shocked. In my most ungracious moments, I was also selfishly relieved that it wasn't me that had to receive this news about my family. I was relieved that it wasn't my brother who died and that I didn't have to feel the pit of pain that death brings to those who are still living. I would move the earth to help Tina. I would stand by her side indefinitely, hold her hand, cry with her, or cry for her if she needed. I would help her make plans and laugh and listen. If she wanted, I would speak on her behalf at the funeral. I love her like my own sister, and I grieved with her and her family, but I am still a selfish person who would do anything not to be her.

I think when a person dies, we look for a prayer or talisman that will keep death away. At Tina's sister's funeral, I whispered this pact to myself:

"I will stand by my friend in need on this day. I will sacrifice a goat, wear a necklace of beads, paint a cross on my door; I will recite an incantation that wards off evil spirits. Please, God, or Buddha, or whatever the hell is out there, I will do whatever it takes not to be her. Please let me live another day without death at my door."

To the outside world I pretend I am a rock, but inwardly I am a fearful soul who would like nothing more than to have death just take a day off.

This is crazy, because we all die, but in North America we pretend that people don't. We pretend that doctors or miracles or both will save us. We watch movies about the exception to the rule, people who escape death or die for a few minutes and come back to life. This is a distortion of reality. For every miracle we read about or see on the Internet, there are countless unmiracles where people don't beat the odds. Books about people who have glimpsed life after death, like *Proof of Heaven* by Eben Alexander; a memoir about a neurosurgeon recounting his near-death experience during a coma and *Heaven Is for Real - A Little Boy's Astounding Story of His Trip to Heaven and Back* by Todd Burpo with Lynn Vincent that have each spent weeks on the *New York Times* best seller list. We read these stories of incredible hope and joy, but there's no mistaking that our friends, family, and colleagues slip away from us for a myriad of reasons that we can't fix or change. There's no goal sheet with action steps that will keep us from dying.

When I find out from friends or colleagues that someone has died, the first question I want to scream is, "How did they die?" I want to shake the answer out of them, but I don't. I wait until they start to unfold details. I wait until there might be a proper moment to subtly, politely ask how it happened. I do not have a morbid curiosity about the details of the person's death, but I am seeking a critical piece of information that I use to continue to breathe. When I read about a young person's death in the newspaper or online—especially if it's a child, a husband, or a mother of three in her early forties—I scour the article for details about the circumstances of the death. My unsubstantiated theory goes like this: the more information I have, the better I can calculate the odds of my own death or the odds of anyone in my family dying. This is my way of rationalizing some of my fears about death. With every detail of the death revealed, I file it under one of two categories:

1. This could never be me.

2. This could be me.

Example: *Female political activist dies skydiving when parachute fails to open. Foul play is suspected.*

Let's review how this would apply to me.

Female: Check.

Political activist: Not likely.

Skydiving: No, thanks.

Failing parachute: Who would put that much faith in a giant piece of nylon at twenty thousand feet?

Foul play: The only person who wants to hurt me is my bookkeeper, because wads of receipts in an envelope make her mildly murderous.

Likelihood of death in this manner: Zero. Other than my being a female, this is never going to happen to me.

Example: *Mother of three dies suddenly at home. Foul play has been ruled out, and since there is no apparent trauma, the medical experts are hypothesizing a possible brain aneurysm.*

There is no need for an analysis here. She's a mom who died at home from a silent, bulging blood vessel that burst in her brain. These deaths make me sweat. These deaths give me the life shiver. The odds of this happening to me are still very small, but now I add aneurysm to the growing list of fear-based death thoughts that drift in the periphery of my subconscious. There's a long list of potential death options, but I just keep reminding myself of the slim odds that any of them will happen to my husband, my children, or myself. This rationalization allows me to go on with doing the laundry, packing lunches, and buying groceries where, without the imminent possibility of death, these things matter.

In the End

I'm not sure whether the pain of losing someone close to you ever really goes away. The pain might lessen, or fade but it doesn't mean we don't wonder what it would be like if they hadn't died, if we could have one more minute to say "Goodbye," "I'm sorry," or "I love you." People say that when your child or your spouse dies, you don't grieve and then stop, you only cope. Like Bonanno says, you cope because there is only coping, and there is only learning to live with a new normal.

It's been over twenty years since my dad died, and of course the pie is no longer a circle filled entirely with me. My pie is filled with experiences both fantastic and sad, and my spiritual slice is splintered by what I have learned and what I still need to understand. My dad's death was a gift that allowed me to see, at such a young age, how life is an amazing experience. It gave me the courage to ask "Why not?" when it came to making decisions that were not mainstream or universally liked. My dad's passing gave me a window to a type of spiritualism that is only opened by living in the moment, by breathing in experiences, and sometimes by swimming against the current. Death sucks, but it gives me the strength and fortitude to remember why life is worth living.

Oh Death, you remind me to love those around me. You teach me respect for myself and others. You breathe compassion into me for those who suffer more or live harder than I do. But most importantly, you give me perspective—perspective on what matters, perspective on my judgments, and perspective on my patience. Death, you are a sobering reminder to me that spiritualism is not about following a prescribed dogma, but about being present in the moment.

Call this slice spiritualism, tranquility, awareness, or oneness, but it is the one piece of pie that can give me vision when it's needed the most.

Korol a double winner

Twelve Mississauga
Federation of Schools
Championship held at
Classified as one of
Championships attrac
areas and 750 high sch
Leading the Missis
Heather Korol, who ju
"I expected to win h
nice to win two golds i
Korol completed the
conds to finish first a
and Scarborough's Ja
It was in the senior
medal with a jump of
place Audrey Llewell
the standard for comp
in Argentina.
Taking third-place i
St. Paul's student Em
earn bronze.
Rudan, who was a
Regional championsh
tion to a bronze medal
the triple jump to take
Other Mississauga
earned silver in the
(silver, junior girls' t
nior girls' 80-m hurdle
midget girls' 100-m)
400-m), St.Martins' W
plewood's Charlie Hu
Just missing the m
nior boys' high jump)
Erindale's Andrew R
Canfield (fourth, juni
in the midget girls' tri

Our

This week's Athle
honors go to Applew
Heather Korol.
Korol, a Grade 13 s
gold medals at last
Federation of Schools
ciation (OFSAA) T
Championships and w
placing Mississaugan

Golden girl Heather Korol was in winning form at the OFSAA Track and Field Championships held over the weekend. The Applewood Heights student won the senior girls' long jump and hurdles events resulting in her being named our Athlete of the Week.

Article from the Mississauga News 1989. Bottom right inset picture:
My dad on a day pass from the hospital, sitting against the fence, watching me "fly".

PART IV

Just A Slice

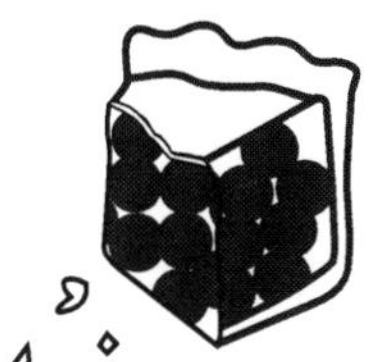

CHAPTER SIXTEEN

* * *

A Slice of Happy

I don't know if feminism will lead the charge for women seeking both a vibrant career and a balanced family slice. I'm not sure that without a dramatic shift in our food culture, losing weight, and eating right will ever be easy and I don't know if a struggling relationship can get past tired arguments and lost love through counseling. I do know that whatever circumstances you are facing, you will be happier if you focus on one slice at a time.

The Internet is filled with viral posts that expound happy clichés being forwarded and shared repeatedly. While you might not cover your office walls in *Believe* posters, most people want and need to be reminded that life is filled with inspiring, incredible experiences. Whether you dream about hiking the West Coast Trail, publishing a book, acting in the theatre, or joining a charitable organization, these life experiences bring us new perspectives, and a renewed spirit for living our lives like the poster guy rappelling off the edge of a cliff. There will always be competing forces pulling you in different directions, but if you can wade through the noise and pick one slice to focus on, you may find that all the slices feel a bit more full. Finding your slice of happy is about taking a step back and truly seeing what is important to you. It's about looking at all that you could do and picking one thing you want to do.

The Big Picture

Advice is always easier said than done. Life is filled with complications and unexpected obstacles, and even when your intentions are rock solid, things go wrong or don't go the way you expected. This is an inevitable part of reaching for new goals. When "life" happens it's important to remember the one directive that may keep you going: find perspective.

Around the world, people have the same universal desires and needs: they need healthy bodies, they need ideas that engage their mind, and they need something to be passionate about. Our three states of being: body, mind, soul and our nine slices of pie: health, wealth, career, friends, family, spirituality, sex, leisure, and community all need to be kept in perspective. A rock climber may see life or death in the placement of a rope securing piton. A health care worker knows that having the flu can be an inconvenience for some or a death sentence for others. And an astronaut can see our world as a magnificent planet filled with natural wonders or as an inconspicuous dot against the vastness of the universe. Perspective brings meaning to our actions and reactions. Taking a moment to see or feel the world from someone else's viewpoint may give you an opportunity to change your own perspective. I remind myself that whatever goal I'm working on or struggle I am facing perspective will be the greatest tool I have.

Poker Body

I know a secret about my husband. He's never actually told me, and I don't think he even knows about it himself. My husband has a tell.

A tell is a sign or repeated physical motion that alerts others to an emotional shift within a person. It's an unconscious action that reveals something you don't want anyone to see outwardly. In the game of poker, a tell could be a facial tick or an unintentional finger tap on the table when a player has a good hand.

My husband's tell is probably not unique, except for the consistency in how it appears.

"Heather, I want to show you this video." Mark had his iPhone ready to upload a YouTube video to our TV in the living room.

"Okay. I know how you love YouTube, but I don't want to watch TV." I was feeling overwhelmed by the sheer volume of things that needed to get done and stopping to watch a YouTube video just made me feel annoyed.

"No, you're going to like this."

"Just to be clear, nothing is going to jump out at me on the screen with a loud screeching noise, right?" I hate that. I detest those e-mails that tell you to watch closely or see if you can spot the flying squirrel, and then—*whammo!*—a screaming skull pops out at you. I drink too much coffee for those things to be okay.

"No, no screeching monsters."

"Okay, and no yucky accidents either, right?" Watching a guy crack his head open when he falls off his skateboard while riding on a handrail above concrete stairs without a helmet makes my stomach hurt. It also makes me think they are stupid.

"No, none of that. It if helps, I don't like those things either."

"Fine. How long is it?" The litany of questions I asked was longer than the amount of time it would have taken to watch the video three times over.

"Come on, I've known you long enough that I think I know what you like."

"Yeah. Do you know I'm allergic to kiwi?" I was taking the conversation down a rabbit hole. A place where an unsuspecting husband is lured into a conversation that ultimately ends with, "Do you really care about me?"

"No, but we never eat kiwi."

"Exactly. The sides of my cheeks go tingly, and my tongue feels prickly all day."

"But you won't die." He efficiently dismissed my kiwi concern by stating the logical outcome.

"No, I won't die." My tone implied he should still care.

"But if you eat kiwi and your mouth goes prickly, how would I know?"

"I don't know. I was waiting to see if you would ever ask me if I was allergic to anything. Like, your love for me is so great that you need to know everything about me."

"I do know everything about you. Please stop so we can watch this video."

"Fine. I'll watch the video." Somehow in the last few years, YouTube has become the post-dinner entertainment of men everywhere. Scotch, CrossFit, and YouTube videos—the rugged urban man's guide to happiness.

"Here it is." I could tell by its more than one million views that it had already started its viral ascent.[25] It opened with images of security cameras—cameras on top of buildings, cameras on overpasses, and hidden cameras on busy streets. In just over a minute, the video showed a montage of amazing, powerful images that were caught and digitized by security cameras around the world. No one died, no one got hurt, and no one jumped out of the screen and yelled in my face. Instead, there were clips of a couple stealing a kiss in Rome, a quick-thinking man who pushed a stalled car off a railway crossing before it was hit by a train, a man racing after a woman to return her wallet that had dropped on the sidewalk, and two friends tackling each other in a best-friend, wide-grinned bro-hug. The short montage captured moments in which people were acting like people—doing the human thing instead of the thinking thing. They were reacting to life's fear, joy, love, and humor. The cameras captured honest, instantaneous reactions that couldn't be mistaken for someone pretending.

As the video ended, I glanced over at my husband. He was wearing shorts, and I could see goose bumps on his legs. I breathed out one word: "Wow."

This was a quiet "wow," because I realized that what I had watched was not just a heart-warming compilation of nice deeds, but a refreshing perspective on human nature.

“I thought you’d like it. I was thinking about your book and how you asked me to help you with ideas for your seminar. The video reminded me of how you like to show people a different perspective. You see things differently – you have an eye for honesty. Even when you joke about stuff, I know there is a caring, soft person under all that protective hardness.”

I was speechless. My husband had silenced me in that moment. I looked down at his leg, and I could see his tell. His goose bumps were revealing his emotional truth.

“Thank you, honey. This is perfect.”

He leaned over and gave me a kiss. As he did, my hand touched his leg. It felt like prickly corrugated paper. It was bumpy and sharp, with little hairs that were sticking up. Then he was off. He left the couch, put on his shoes, and scuttled outside to do some backyard fixing.

Everyone gets goose bumps, but Mark’s are a secret signal to me. The more he is touched by something, the bigger the bumps; the more joy he feels, the longer they last. He could be watching one of the girls pick up a frog for the first time and her squeals of delight will make my husband’s leg pebble up like the Sierra Valley foothills. His physical reaction, his tell reminds me that even when work deadlines, family obligations, and revolving kid viruses are staring me in the face, there is always some small piece or moment in the day that is going well. He helps me keep my perspective.

Interleukin Mind

One day, science exploded my head.

“There are a group of cells called interleukin cells.” I was sitting in Microbiology 332. I was in my third year of university working towards my science degree. The professor was starting on a rather dry topic about cells that react to one another.

“As you can see, the interleukin family is a group of beta trefoil cytokines. They play a central role in the regulation of immune and inflammatory responses." There were seventeen different interleukin cell types, but number six made me look up from my doodle page.

"Interleukin-6 is most known for its cooperation with the IgE family. These are the group of cells that produce the fiercest of reactions in response to allergies and anaphylaxis." Whenever I listen to science mumbo-jumbo, I like to dumb it down as if I were Dora the Explorer talking to Boots about finding the tall mountain. I use little steps so the story unfolds slowly. It went like this: IgE cells are the ones that trigger your body to make mucus. I call them the snot cells. When your snot cells get all crazy, it shows up as an allergy. When your snot cells are really messed up, they trigger a response that can kill you.

With the prevalence and media attention of people dying from allergies related to eating nuts or shellfish, the phrase "anaphylactic shock" is now common speak. There are enough kids in school wearing EpiPen injectors in little belt pouches to make you wonder whether the human race will make it.

The professor went on to explain that the snot cells have a special baby-helper cell. The baby-helper is the only cell in the snot family that can cross the placenta and protect an unborn baby from other harmful cells.[26]

Whoa. I looked around to see if anyone else heard this. Most students were dozing or taking some form of notes as Professor Cell continued his monologue. What made me pause, was hearing about a microscopic world in which one specific cell is given the job of keeping tiny babies healthy before they become loud, screaming, keep-you-up-all-night babies. Was I the only one that thought this was incredible? One cell that helps manage babies in utero because the other billion cells have their own super-specific job. There I was, twenty-one years old, three years into a degree in molecular science, studying evolution and the process by which cells absorb other cells to become more complex, asking the timeless question, "How did we get here?" It had only just dawned on me that every cell in the human body has a specific and complicated job and they all work together in a microscopic world that we know almost nothing about.

Like millions before me, I question how we ever came to be on this earth and how we've managed to survive this long. Why is there one cell so specific that it's the only type that can visit a baby in utero while the others can't? Why is the body made up of billions more bacteria than healthy cells? Why do our cells get confused and attack themselves? Science is only just scratching the surface that might unveil the quantum leap required to understand the secrets of the universe. I realized the more I learned, the less I knew.

Everyday I am humbled by some new bit of information that scientists have uncovered about our universe and each time it feels like 'perspective to infinity' and it's simply mind-blowing.

Fire Soul

Some people say we have a soul or a spirit, some people use words like, essence, life force, *prana*, or *chi*, and if none of these suit your taste, call it your passion. Whatever is not your body or your mind is the leftover part that defines you as *you*. It's this third state of being that I feel offers me the greatest level of perspective.

I have a friend that I call Bunny, because she runs like a rabbit. She's a twig with hamstrings, and I'm guessing she weighs ninety-five pounds with work boots on. I'm entirely certain that she doesn't own a pair of work boots, because she's a little more Neiman Marcus than Kodiak Outlet, but she's fun and honest and easy to be around. I met her a year after Mark and I had our third baby and we had just moved to a new town.

Bunny is nice. She is the type of person that would sit and listen to a long story told by an uninteresting person. She's sweet and kind, and she has a sparkly energy underneath her demure head nods and expensive highlights.

The first time she called to ask if I wanted to head out for a run with her, I let her know I don't want to run competitively; I just wanted to get out of the house and enjoy the company of another woman (even if that other woman is really thin). She agreed and we met at the local trailhead.

We started our jog on a dirt trail surrounded by a wooded area. "Why did you move here?" I asked the first question so that she would have to do all the talking while I breathed like I was in labor.

"You know, Lance and I needed a break from the city. He was struggling with the commute. It felt like we were getting so busy, and then more and more things became about keeping up with the neighbors."

"I hear you." I kept it short. Navigating the twisty trails already had me winded.

"Yeah, we've had our struggles," Bunny said as she hopped over one of the rocky outcroppings on the trail.

Over the years I've learned to hold back a bit when I'm getting to know someone. I can be real and honest, but I don't have to shock friends on the 'first date' with comments like "I think circumcisions are barbaric" or "I really like watching *South Park*, don't you?" I searched for the right words to convey that I understood that her use of the word, "struggle" was a possible can of worms. I decided if she wanted to talk more, I was there to listen.

"Oh, yeah?" It was a question-statement that acknowledged she might want to share, but I wasn't going to push her. I left it open for her to decide how much she wanted to reveal.

"It took us a long time to have our kids." She seemed hesitant about getting into this heavy conversation as we picked our way along the trail at the edge of the escarpment. She and Lance had two children very near in age to my two oldest girls. Where Mark could pretty much sneeze with his pants off and I was pregnant, I'd had many conversations over the years with people trying desperately to have kids.

Bunny continued, "I should say that we didn't have trouble getting pregnant. We just couldn't stay pregnant." She bounced along like Tigger as our conversation entered the baby zone.

"Oh, wow. That *is* shitty." Having had three healthy babies, and never having any trouble getting pregnant or staying pregnant, I could relate in only a limited way. Some days Mark and I cursed our rampant fertility, but stories like these always made us thankful that we could have children easily.

"It turns out I have a rare autoimmune disease that clots the blood in my placenta," Bunny explained. She knew about my science background, and she felt comfortable giving me the technical details.

"Oh, wow, that sucks. So you didn't have a problem getting pregnant, but you couldn't carry the babies?" My mind raced and my stomach tightened. What could be worse than that? Was it worse if you could never get pregnant, or was it worse that every time you got pregnant you lost the baby? There was no answer to this question. There was just nothing comforting I could think to say.

"We tried so many different things. Eventually we found a specialist who was able to help us have Emma and Alex."

The conversation drifted into the multiple ways they tried to stay pregnant and the different drugs she took and tests she participated in. All I could think of was that this woman, little Bunny, suffered countless miscarriages and the repeated heartache and pain of losing her babies. It's one thing to talk about it later, after you've had two healthy children, but I was certain it was another to have lived it.

As she jogged along, I could see the years of struggle written on her face. We took a wrong turn on the trail and circled back around to the trail markers that would take us toward the car. We slowed to a walk, and she turned to me.

"I was sitting at a coffee shop while I was waiting to get the ultrasound results of another failing pregnancy, and I was looking out a window that faced the street. As I sat there, I watched everyone walk by, some with babies, some without. Old, young, alone, with friends and without, I watched them all. As I looked at them, I wanted to ask: Why me? Why is this happening to me? Why am I losing these pregnancies? Is it me? Is it Lance? Is it God? As I sat there alone, tears streaming down my face, trying to sip a coffee, I came to understand that everyone has their own fire. Everyone has a fire they have to walk through. They may not be trying to get pregnant, but every one of those people outside the window has something. Heather, it's not *if* you will walk through the fire, it's *when.*"

She took a breath and continued.

"I wanted to ask those people in the street, 'What is your fire? Have you had it yet?' because my fire felt like a very long and forever feeling. I found myself in a dark place that was hard to get out of, but seeing those people outside the window, I knew I wasn't alone. Everyone goes through it at some point, because it's not if, it's when."

I didn't ask how many times she miscarried, because it didn't matter. She had struggled through her own personal hell, and now she was finding her way back to a new normal. She put her own pain in perspective by thinking and knowing she was not the only one—not the only one to face a personal tragedy that put her soul on hold.

The human spirit is a tenacious part of each of us. Our capacity to heal and gain life perspective means that touching your soul is part of the answer to finding your happiness. To walk into the fire is to feel loss and suffering, but to walk through the fire is to find your strength, resolution, and love.

Goose bumps, interleukin, and fire—body, mind, and soul are all parts of the same whole that make up 'you.' When I crawl into bed at night, long after my husband has gone to sleep, I lie down like a ninja, but he always knows I'm there. He sneaks over to my side to press up against me. He wraps his arms around me and I feel him sink into me and relax as we fall asleep. In his previous job as a police officer and his current job as a firefighter, he sees death on a regular basis, and occasionally he gets the opportunity to save someone's life. His perspective is different from mine. He sees a much sharper image of the thread we straddle between living and dying. When he wraps his arms around me every night, I believe he thinks that if he holds me tight enough, I will always be there. If for some reason one of us didn't wake up in the morning, he would have made sure our last moments together were that dreamy, perfect feeling that life is good. His actions touch my soul and they remind me to keep the perspective that I always talk about, to find the calm in my storm and the love in my heart.

Just a Slice

If I could prove that 'having it all' was scientifically impossible, people would still try and that's okay, because learning, exploring, and reaching for something more are essential parts of living. If you stopped trying to move forward, if you tossed in the towel on personal growth, life would feel like you were standing still. Alternatively, running endlessly toward an unmarked finish line or competing in the detrimental life-comparison race erodes your ability to enjoy the great moments you *do* have. I know I am happier when I choose compassion over judgment, perspective over comparison, and I am happier since I stopped trying to have it all and just picked a slice.

When you set about picking your own slice it could be as simple as feeling like your health or your career slice is the one you *should* focus on, but this may not be the case. I ask you to trust that voice, the one inside you that screams for your attention. Don't pick the "should" slice, pick the one that speaks to you from your soul, your passion. Pick the slice that will make you happier on many levels. There will always be more than one slice vying for your attention but the one that makes your stomach tingle and your mouth go dry is the one you should start with. Even when your logical brain is telling you that volunteering time in the community is not going to help your career or that you should work on your health even though your heart is yelling at you to paint a mural size picture for your living room – this is the voice you should heed. Picking a slice is not about having it all, but uncompromisingly enjoying the one you do have.

You have to decide what will make you happier. Is it finding more time to spend with your children? Is it leaving friends who don't share your personal goals and dreams? Is it grabbing the person you love most and holding them so close you can feel their heart beating with yours?

My career has been a shooting star and a fizzling backyard sparkler; my marriage is filled with love and ambivalence, all in the same hour; my kids are my supreme joy and my daily torture; my health is my breath and my fat all rolled up in one; my wealth is overly abundant and withering away on the same money tree; my community is my looking glass to the future and my Achilles' heel; my leisure holds both my passions and my vices; and my spiritualism is all of the grandest hopes and greatest fears that I have in this life. Without perspective, my life would be a lot less enjoyable.

The advice in this book is simple: Pick a slice and dive in. Meditate yourself silly; drink coffee and wine with friends until they feel like family; hug your kids as much as they will let you; eat, move, sleep, and breathe with grace every day; have sex with abandon; laugh till you cry; use love, respect, and compassion as actions instead of just words and above all else, add perspective daily.

Finding a slice of happy *is* the answer to having the whole pie.

ACKNOWLEDGMENTS

This book *is* my Oscar-pie. If you could see me, you would know that I am holding my book wrapped tight in one hand raised above my head with the podium microphone in the other. It is on these pages that I will give my acceptance speech because really, an acknowledgement page is more accurately a giant thank you to all those that helped me along the way.

To my husband, the strong, wonderful man that keeps my toes warm, allows me to rest easy at night, and brings my life the greatest sense of fulfillment with our bond—I thank you with all my heart. To my daughters, Clara, Ellie, and Fiona you are my little baby angels that are the extensions of my soul. I love you and I thank you for your patience every night when you asked me if I would be coming to bed and I'd say, "Not yet, honey, I'm just going to work on the book."

To my mom Gail, or 'Gigi' as my three girls call her. My mom came to life in this book during the story of her tea towel obsession but she is so much more than a person that likes tchotchkes. My mom is the person that watched my kids when I just couldn't handle another minute of interruptions. She is the rock that patiently waits behind me, solid and warm from the sun, while I lean back and rest my soul against her on this journey to raise a family, love my spouse, run a business and take on the relentless task or writing, editing and creating a book. She believes in the slice and she has given me the breath I need some days to bring this idea to the finish line. I love you mom.

To Tina Comi, my BFF and the brilliant author of *Till Dance Do Us Part.* Tina is the Oprah to my Gail and some days it's the reverse. We started this book-writing journey together and we are finishing our books at the same time. I could never have made it through this maddening process without her. There were days she literally begged me to finish a chapter, a sentence, an edit, or rewrite. We have cried and cursed our way through the process. We have applauded and encouraged each other's mini successes. My days would be darker without my best friend in my corner sending me love or lending an ear. Tina, you are the wind beneath these sometimes exhausted wings that would a need a spray-tan and liposuction if this really were Oscar night. Life is better with a best friend and I'm pretty sure we are two halves of a whole person. Thank goodness we found each other because (sweep index fingers in a small circle) you complete me.

There were many written sections that ended up on the edited pile, the story about my brother Chris, who was paramount in getting my first business off the ground. He sent me my first client and couldn't understand why I thought running a business was a crazy idea. He said I would be a natural at it and he was right. He also told me to buy Apple stocks fifteen years ago, but who listens to their brother all the time? Thank you May and Chris for all your help through the years including; being an awesome Auntie and Uncle to my kids, attending to my lawyerly issues and saving my files from the blue screen of death countless times.

Donna Arnold, who has the patience of Job and is always there when we need her help. My second mom is a strong woman that raised four of her own children and lovingly cares for every one of her ten grandchildren. Thank you for helping us get through countless ESAR, RockstAR, and Trek or Treat events and allowing me to use a bit of your life story.

Marissa Schroder, who has been an incredible influence. Who knew there would another women so fantastic that she would be like a little key that opened a locked door when I needed it the most? Thank you for your advice, encouragement, great conversations and marketing expertise. I love that together we can pick up where we left off without missing a beat. Thank you for all your help on this journey.

Hillary Lutes has a special place in my heart for all her work over the years. It's tough being my personal assistant; some days there could be no worse job. Her ability to complete all menial and major tasks without balking, her incredible sense of humor and our shared love of chocolate and all things delightful to eat has made the years growing the business and raising little babies a thousand times easier. Hurry Hillary, there are people that need to see your beauty and hear your words in the world—don't wait another minute to go for what you want.

Thank you to Marg Scheben-Edey for the perfect insight on the first read-through; your words of wisdom were exactly what I needed to move to the next step. Thank you Robin Colucci for your mystical and practical coaching on getting the first draft out and teaching me what it means to edit, so I could face the horror of endless second, third, and fourth draft revisions. Thank you, Eric Anderson for your round of edits and suggestions on moving forward in this process as well as Sarah Stewart for her final content edit and proofread. Stephanie Whitesell for assuring me that there were some funny parts and wondering if she was one of the "organized people" that I referred to in chapter two that made me crazy...um, no of course not! Kathy Carter, for her insightful edits and her meticulous attention to detail. Kathy in her gentle way guided me to ensuring there was one consistent message in this book. Without her continual questioning of the thesis of this book I'm not sure I would have worked so hard to find the answer.

A giant thank you to Sherry Lemcke for her beautiful cover photo and her tireless attitude for getting the cover image just right. Not only did she take the photo of the pie – she actually baked it, cut it, and sent me photos along the way! Her brilliance is in her vision. Sherry has an eye for all things creative, including fonts, lighting, spacing and general coolness. If you are ever in need a photographer that gets it, this woman is *über* talented and a true gem to work with.

There is also a short list of people that have influenced my life in a way that brought me to a new level: Steve Caws, as my track and field coach, Claude Church, who lent me and my husband the book, *The 22 Immutable Laws of Marketing*, and changed the way we approached our business. Ken Broaderip, who continually hired me for speaking engagements as he moved through his own corporate career. Frank Mule, for always supporting my work as a speaker and trainer. Janet Whitney, who is still a great influence and friend in my life. Thank you Michele Smeh for helping me find a second home at CrossFit Mozomo and Jen Fawcett and her incredible spirit and the coming work we will do together. Thank you Ed Arnold for my favorite chair that I've spent countless hours in, semi-reclined editing the hard copy of this book. Thank you Sarah Livingston for keeping me sane every Jan 31st with your gentle reminders to send you my "other books". To Carol Parks and Andrea Parks for sharing my blogs around the country and around the globe. A special thank you to my top-shelf Facebook and Twitter followers, Stew-the-bass-man, Margie Schurman, Petra Uu, and Judie Predko, Kelly McNichol, and Jamie Elliot. Thank you Helena Hadfield for the compliment that, *I was the best personal trainer in the world* and for retweeting a blog post I wrote about your husband that sent my website stats, into the stratosphere.

A special thank you to all my friends that allowed me to use their stories or photos and have supported me on this long and winding road: Liz, Trevor, Paige and Owen Masson; Manda and Adam Price; Ken and Esther Tursley; Bonnie and Doug Chisholm; Sarah and Jeff Inglis; Andrea and George Savard; Rachael and Doug Wilkinson; Drew Dancey; Greg Williams; Scott Morrison; Vinson Lee; Gordon Brown; Ira Kargel; Kevin Wallace; Cathy Gallagher; Andrea Hutt-Good; Patty VanLiefland; Meg Mancuso; Maria Faria; Laurie Novak; Denise Buffet; Michelle, Brian, Brianna, Tim, and Sarah Arnold.

I'm sure the music has already come up and they are fading to commercial. Writing a book is a collective process. Thank you to all those (including those I'm certain to have forgotten) that helped me along the way.

If you'd like Heather to speak at your book club, writer's group or next event, drop her an email, she'd love to hear from you.

To reach Heather:

www.asliceofhappy.com
www.heatherkorol.com
www.heathersgym.com

Like A Slice of Happy on Facebook at:
https://www.facebook.com/ASliceOfHappy?ref=hl

Like Heather's Gym on Facebook at:
https://www.facebook.com/gymheather?ref=hl On Twitter: @sliceofhappy

By email: mailto:heather@heatherkorol.com?subject=Email from A Slice of Happy ebook.

CITATIONS:

1 "$11 Billion Self-Improvement Market Moves Online," *PRWeb,* December 1 2010, http://www.prweb.com/releases/2010/12/prweb4847314.htm

2 Bob Hirshon. "Adaptive Happiness," *ScienceNetLinks,* July 14 2006, http://sciencenetlinks.com/science-news/science-updates/adapative-happiness/

3 "Martin Luther King, Jr. Quotes," *Think Exist,* http://thinkexist.com/quatation/occasionally_in_life_are_those_moments_of/324620.html http://www.nobelprize.org/nobel_prizes/peace/laureates/1964/king-lecture.html.

4 Anne-Marie Slaughter. "Why Women Still Can't Have it All," *The Atlantic,* June 13 2012, http://www.theatlantic.com/magazine/archive/2012/07/why-women-still-cant-have-it-all/309020/

5 Daily Mail Reporter. "Aged 33? Then you won't have time to read this as it's the busiest period of your life," *Daily Mail Online,* November 1 2010, http://www.dailymail.co.uk/news/article-1325431/Aged-33-Then-wont-time-read-busiest-period-life.html

6 Leo Babauta. "Zen Habits Frequently Asked Questions (FAQS)," *Zen Habits,* February 1 2010, http://zenhabits.net/faq/

7 Sheryl Sandberg. *Lean In: Women, Work and the Will to Lead.* (Toronto: Random House of Canada, 2013), 839, Kindle e-book.

8 "Divorce Statistics." *Divorce Statistics,* http://www.divorcestatistics.org/

9 Ty Kiisel. "Does Anyone Really Take Mommy Bloggers Seriously?" *Forbes,* December 21 2011, http://www.forbes.com/sites/tykiisel/2011/12/21/does-anyone-really-take-mommy-bloggers-seriously/

10 Bill Hendrick. "Percentage of Overweight, Obese Americans swells," *WebMD Health News,* February 10 2010, http://www.webmd.com/diet/news/20100210/percentage-of-overweight-obese-americans-swells

11 Daniel J. DeNoon. "Sleep Less, Get Diabetes?" *WebMD Health News,* August 12 2009, http://diabetes.webmd.com/news/20090812/sleep-less-get-diabetes

12 Michele Simon. "A Guide to Food Industry Front Groups: How Corporate Lobbyists Control Public Discourse," *EcoWatch,* May 22 2013, http://ecowatch.com/2013/food-industry-front-groups-lobbyists-control-public-discourse/

13 Andrew Seibert, ed. "Life Stages With Ulcerative Colitis," *WebMD,* October 24 2012, http://www.webmd.com/ibd-crohns-disease/ulcerative-colitis-10/uc-problem-foods.
Jennie Harrell. "What's Wrong With Legumes?" *Easy Paleo,* September 30 2011, http://www.easypaleo.com/2011/09/30/whats-wrong-with-legumes/

14 Annals of Internal Medicine. "Insufficient Sleep Undermines Dietary Efforts to Reduce Adiposity," October 5, 2010, http://annals.org/article.aspx?articleid=746184

15 ANI Agency. "Men think about sex 34 times each day and women 18 times," *dna,* August 13 2013, http://www.dnaindia.com/lifestyle/1873799/report-men-think-about-sex-34-times-each-day-and-women-18-times

16 "The 'Lifestyle' -- Real-Life Wife Swaps," ABC News, March 18 2005, http://abcnews.go.com/2020/Health/story?id=2395727&page=1&singlePage=true
http://www.swingfesteventsmedia.com/TheLifestyle.htm

17 Christopher Ryan and Cacilda Jetha. *Sex at Dawn: How We Mate, Why We Stray, and What It Means for Modern Relationships.* (Harper Perennial, 2012), Kindle e-book.

18 Jenny Dolph. "Michigan man tries to sell kidney on ebay," *ABC 57 News,* December 22 2011, http://www.abc57.com/news/crime/Michigan-man-tries-to-sell-kidney-on-ebay-136091938.html

19 Ibid.

20 Roger Highfield. "Relative wealth makes you happier," Nov. 22, 2007. http://www.telegraph.co.uk/science/science-news/3315638/Relative-wealth-makes-you-happier.html

21 Ibid.

22 Beth Teitell. "Racing to Find Donors," *boston.com,* April 10 2012, http://www.boston.com/sports/marathon/articles/2012/04/10/boston_marathon_charity_runners_race_to_meet_fund_raising_goal/

23 Ibid.

24 Ibid.

25 Coca-Cola, *Coca-Cola Security Cameras,* YouTube video, 1:32 minutes, posted June 11 2012, http://www.youtube.com/watch?v=auNSrt-QOhw

26 "Immunoglobulin G." *Wikipedia,* last modified July 31 2013, http://en.wikipedia.org/wiki/Immunoglobulin_G

Made in the USA
Lexington, KY
23 November 2014